MW01097224

The Origin of the Milky Way

& Other Living Stories of the Cherokee

The Origin of the Milky Way

✳

& Other Living Stories of the Cherokee

Collected and edited by

BARBARA R. DUNCAN

With stories told by

DAVY ARCH, ROBERT BUSHYHEAD,
EDNA CHEKELELEE, MARIE JUNALUSKA,
KATHI LITTLEJOHN, & FREEMAN OWLE

Illustrations by SHAN GOSHORN

The University of North Carolina Press
CHAPEL HILL

This book was published with the assistance of the Blythe Family Fund of the University of North Carolina Press.

© 2008
The University of
North Carolina Press
Illustrations © Shan Goshorn
All rights reserved
Designed and typeset in Trump
Mediaeval and ITC Obelisk by
Kim Bryant and Eric M. Brooks
Manufactured in the United
States of America

Cover art: Shan Goshorn
(Eastern Band Cherokee),
www.shangoshorn.com

The paper in this book meets
the guidelines for permanence
and durability of the Committee
on Production Guidelines for
Book Longevity of the Council
on Library Resources.
The University of North Carolina
Press has been a member of the
Green Press Initiative since 2003.

Library of Congress
Cataloging-in-Publication Data
The origin of the Milky Way and
other living stories of the Cherokee /
collected and edited by Barbara R.
Duncan ; with stories told by Davy
Arch . . . [et al.] ; illustrations by
Shan Goshorn.
    p. cm.
Includes bibliographical references.
ISBN 978-0-8078-3219-6 (cloth : alk.
paper)—ISBN 978-0-8078-5930-8
(pbk. : alk. paper)
1. Cherokee Indians—Folklore.
2. Tales—North Carolina.
3. Storytellers—North Carolina.
I. Duncan, Barbara R. II. Arch, Davy.
E99.C5O75 2008
398.08997′25—dc22

                        2008015676

A Caravan book.
For more information, visit
www.caravanbooks.org.

cloth   12 11 10 09 08
         5 4 3 2 1
paper 12 11 10 09 08
         5 4 3 2 1

University of North Carolina Press books may be purchased at a discount for
educational, business, or sales promotional use. For information, please visit
www.uncpress.unc.edu or write to UNC Press, attention: Sales Department,
116 South Boundary Street, Chapel Hill, NC 27514-3808.

Contents

The Origin of the Milky Way

& Other Living Stories of the Cherokee

Introduction

Why do people tell stories? For many reasons. Sometimes stories share wisdom about the best way to live. Sometimes stories keep the past alive, or prepare us for the future. Sometimes stories make us laugh, or scare us, or make us wonder about what strange things might happen in the world. But always stories connect us with people—the ones who cared enough to keep the story alive.

The stories in this book have been told by Cherokee people, passed down in spoken words from one generation to the next, for hundreds and perhaps thousands of years. They come from a time when all knowledge was passed on in this form—told orally by one person to another, before the Cherokees used writing. They come from long ago but are still being told today, so I call them living stories. They are also called myths, legends, and folklore.

These stories originated in several different ways. Some were once considered sacred, and told only to certain people, because they explained special knowledge. Those people had to demonstrate that they were worthy of receiving the knowledge before the elders would share it with them. Some stories come from individuals—telling about something that happened to them, or to someone in their family. Other stories tell about supernatural experiences—with ghosts and Little People. And still other stories come from historical events, such as the story of the Trail of Tears.

A number of these stories tell about how to get along with other people, sometimes using animals as characters, to make a point about the right way and the wrong way to act. Other stories tell about origins: how things came to be. Many of them use humor to make their point, though some are very serious. But all Cherokee stories are meant to teach children and remind adults how to live as Cherokees. As you read the stories, you will hear about ideas and beliefs that Cherokee people, over centuries, have considered most important to pass on to their children.

In the old days, stories were told in different settings, as part of life. Some stories were told at home within families. Some stories were told to the whole town, gathered in the townhouse—a large building meant to hold all the members of a community—to pass along news, to tell the history of the people, or just for entertainment. Some stories were told only by medicine people to younger people selected to hear them.

Cherokee stories are unique. Other American Indian tribes have stories that might sound similar, but they are all a little different. You might even see resemblances to stories you have heard from other cultures around the world. But Cherokee stories tell about specific animals, plants, and places in the Cherokees' original homeland in the southern Appalachians, as well as the ideas of Cherokee people over many centuries. The stories' connection to this place, and to the people who have told them for generations, is what makes them special.

Why the Stories Look and Sound the Way They Do

The stories are printed on the page exactly as the Cherokee storytellers say them. They are reproduced word for word, so that you can hear how the Cherokee people sound when they tell the stories. They are written out like poetry, because the storytellers speak rhythmically. If you read them aloud and pause for just a second at the end of each line, you can hear the rhythms of the Cherokee language, even in English.

We speak differently from how we write. Very few people—except maybe your schoolteacher and television news announcers—always use correct English when they are talking. So in these stories, you will find words like "ain't" and sentences that start with "and." We wouldn't do things like that in written English, but that's how the storytellers talk, so their speech is preserved in the stories. You will also find words repeated, such as "and." Storytellers do this to create the rhythm that they like.

How to Pronounce Cherokee Words

In Cherokee language (see the Cherokee translation of "The Origin of the Milky Way" in Chapter 6), consonants are pronounced as in English, and vowels are pronounced as follows:

a   short *a* as in *father*
e   long *a* as in *hay*
i   long *e* as in *me*
o   long *o* as in *over*
u   long *u* as in *rule*
v   nasal *uh* as in *uh-huh*

Learning More about Cherokee People

As you read these stories, you will learn many things about Cherokee people and how they have lived. But it may help to have a few facts before you begin.

Origins of Cherokee people. Cherokee people believe that they have always lived in the southern Appalachians. They believe that the Creator put them there and gave them their language, knowledge, and stories. They believe that the first man and woman lived at Shining Rock (near modern-day Cherokee, North Carolina), and their first town was called Kituhwa.

Archaeologists used to think that all American Indians migrated across the Bering Strait from Asia about 12,500 years ago. Now archaeologists are realizing that people lived in North America and South America long before that. People have lived in the southern Appalachians, the Cherokees' homeland, for more than 14,000 years.

The Cherokees and their ancestors survived for thousands of years in the southern Appalachian Mountains because they knew how to use the plants and animals around them to make everything they needed—food, shelter, clothing, medicine, and weapons. They hunted and fished. They gathered wild plants and then began to cultivate plants. As long as 2,000 years ago, Cherokee men were great warriors and hunters, Cherokee women were great farmers, and Cherokee villages were surrounded by bountiful fields and orchards.

Though many things have changed, Cherokees and other American Indians are still here. The Eastern Band of

Cherokee Indians lives in the mountains of western North Carolina, numbering about 13,000 people. The Cherokee Nation (with more than 250,000 people) and the United Keetoowah Band (about 15,000 people) live in Oklahoma. Many Americans claim descent from Cherokee ancestors.

Food, water, and fire. Cherokees grew, gathered, and hunted for a great variety of food. They considered food a gift from the Creator, and always shared their food with others. Men hunted wild game, such as deer, elk, bison, turkey, and grouse. They hunted smaller birds with blowguns, set traps for turkeys, and shot larger animals with bows and arrows. Cherokees began hunting with guns about 1700.

Men and women also fished for trout and bass. Sometimes a whole village would get in the river and drive fish into a fish trap. Women gathered walnuts, chestnuts, and hickory nuts to eat and put in food. In addition, Cherokee people ate blueberries, blackberries, strawberries, persimmons, and other fruit. Wild greens were eaten as they grew in season: first ramps, then sochan, creasies, wild potatoes, and more. Cherokee women made big gardens, growing corn, beans, squash, pumpkins, and sunflower seeds. The sweetest food Cherokees had was honey locust (the edible pulp of the tree bearing that name), but it was rare. They did not eat milk or sugar or wheat, as we do today, because they did not have cows and did not grow wheat or sugarcane. Most of their food was boiled or roasted. Women made delicious bread and dumplings, something they still do today.

Cherokees believed that it was very important to keep the rivers, creeks, and springs clean. They talked about the river as "The Long Person," *yvwiya gunahita*, with his/her head in the mountains and feet in the ocean. They believed that clean water was necessary for life and also had healing powers, so they never threw garbage or any kind of waste into the rivers. Because of this, they were able to drink from the rivers and springs. Today, the rivers everywhere have been polluted by sewage, waste from factories, and bacteria, so it is not safe to drink from this water any more.

Fire was very important to the Cherokees. One story tells how cold and dark the world was before people got fire. To show respect, Cherokees never threw anything like trash into a fire. Once a year, all the fires in a village were put out except the sacred fire in the townhouse. Then women carried fire from that one central fire, just as the water spider brought fire in the story. This reminded them that fire was a gift, and that they were all one people, starting the new year together. This was part of what was called the Green Corn Ceremony, held when the corn became ripe. If you imagine living without electricity or central heating, you can begin to see why fire was so important: for light, heat, cooking, and survival.

Houses, towns, and government. Cherokee houses were rounded, about 16 x 20 feet in size, with a roof made from slabs of poplar bark rising up to a hole that allowed smoke from inside the house to escape. To make a house, Cherokees stood wooden posts in the ground, about six feet apart, in the shape of the house. Then they cut smaller saplings and wove them around the posts like a basket. Finally, they plastered all of that with clay mud. Sometimes they also plastered the houses white, using mica that made them sparkle.

Women owned the houses. Each family would have a house of the sort just described, as well as a summer house that was like a big porch or arbor, a hot house that was like a sauna, and a house up on stilts for storing corn and other food.

About 1800, Cherokees began building log cabins. Today Cherokee people live in modern houses made of wood, brick, and stone.

The Cherokees' government was based on their towns. Each town had a chief for peace, a chief for war, and a spiritual leader. "Beloved Women" and "Beloved Men," elders who had served the people, also were listened to. The chiefs were elected democratically, by consensus. Everyone had to agree.

People met in the townhouse to discuss issues and elect leaders. Everyone in the village participated: men, women, and children. Everyone had the right to speak. People talked until they agreed on a solution, even if it took days.

At these councils, Cherokees smoked tobacco and other plants in pipes, so that their thoughts would go with the smoke to the Creator, who would hear them. They spoke truthfully, because they believed the Creator was listening.

Cherokees loved their freedom. Both men and women had the right to speak in council, to marry whomever they wanted (outside their clan), and to do what they chose. This freedom worked because each person was also expected to show respect for others and to take responsibility for his or her actions. Adults were expected to put their responsibility to their family before everything else.

Clans. Clans were like big families. You became part of whatever clan your mother belonged to. Cherokees traditionally have seven clans: Long Hair, Paint, Blue, Deer, Bird, Wolf, and Wild Potato. Clans took care of their members and helped enforce Cherokee laws.

Crime and punishment. Children who misbehaved were punished by being told stories that explained how they should act. Or they were ignored. But they were never hit. Such teaching and punishments were usually carried out by their mother's brother, their uncle.

Before the 1800s, Cherokees had just a few laws, and everyone understood them, even people from other tribes. The laws forbade killing someone, selling tribal land, and marrying someone within your own clan. If someone was killed, the victim's clan executed the murderer. If the murderer left town, the victim's clan killed someone from the murderer's clan. In a sense, the clans were responsible for what their members did. Sometimes, a murderer might run to one of the special towns of refuge. If that town let the lawbreaker in, and if he could stay inside the town until the next Green Corn Ceremony, then his crime might be forgiven.

The Cherokees began to have written laws in 1808. Today they have a written constitution and laws, judges, and a tribal police force. Some families still punish and teach their children by telling them stories.

Clothing. In the past, Cherokee clothing was made from woven cloth and tanned hides. American Indians in the Southeast wove bark from mulberry trees into cloth for more than 2,000 years; women wore skirts and capes made from this soft cloth, while men wore shirts made from it.

Men also wore shirts and breechclouts and leggings of cloth or tanned buckskins. Cherokees' toughest moccasins were made of groundhog hide, and their fancy ones were made out of deerskin decorated with porcupine quills, and later beads. Both men and women wore beautiful capes made from the feathers of turkeys and songbirds. On their heads they sometimes wore a bird's wing, or a few feathers. Warriors shaved their heads completely, except for a patch of hair at the crown, which they adorned with feathers and deer hair and shells. (They did not wear feather warbonnets, as did some tribes from the Great Plains—Lakota, Cheyenne, and Crow.)

Today Cherokee people wear blue jeans and T-shirts and running shoes like most people in America. Some of them also have traditional clothing, like that from an earlier time, that they wear for dances, powwows, and special occasions.

Money and trade. Cherokees traded with other tribes for thousands of years. They got pipestone from the Great Lakes, shells from the Gulf of Mexico, and plants from the Atlantic Coast. In turn, mica, soapstone, and copper from the southern Appalachians ended up in all those places.

Beads were traded as well, made from shell, bone, and pottery. Beads made from the shell of the quahog clam were highly valued and traded throughout the area east of the Mississippi River. These white and purple beads, called wampum, were used to make belts that represented treaties between tribes. Sometimes these wampum belts also told stories. The Cherokee word for bead, *adela,* is the word meaning money today.

Getting around. Cherokee runners carried messages between villages, and Cherokee men were very strong runners. Some historical accounts say the men in war parties could run a hundred miles in a day. A surveyor who visited the Cherokees in 1756 said that a man ran alongside the surveyor's horse as it galloped, covering fifty miles in three hours.

Cherokees also had very good trails that went along ridges, over gaps, and beside rivers, and they could draw maps of them. Beginning about 1750, the Cherokees had herds of horses of all colors that they used for traveling, and they bred a small pacing horse with great endurance. But even then, most people walked.

Some of the Cherokee elders alive today remember that people walked everywhere when they were growing up. Some of them walked fifteen miles in one day to go into town, and then walked home again.

Telling time. Before they used clocks and watches, Cherokee people told time during the day by how many hand widths the sun rose above the horizon, with noon being seven hands high. They observed where the sun came up each morning, and how that location changed during the year, so they knew the winter and summer solstices and spring and fall equinoxes, the times when the days are the longest, shortest, and equal to the nights. They also observed monthly changes in the moon, and seasonal changes during the year, according to sunrise, sunset, and the stars. Every month, they observed the moon going from new moon to full to dark and back.

Spiritual beliefs and spirits. Cherokees believed in a creator who made the world. They did not have churches, but they practiced their beliefs every day. Traditionally, they prayed and went to the river every morning at sunrise to "go to water." Singing songs and praying, they immersed themselves in the river in order to wash away any bad thoughts or feelings. They believed water had power to cleanse the body and the spirit. Other ceremonies were a form of praying, and so were some dances. Hunters prayed and gave thanks before and after killing an animal.

Cherokee stories tell about an invisible group of spirits called the Nunnehi. They also talk about Little People, *yvwi tsunsdi*, who are about three feet tall and live throughout the mountains. Some stories describe traveling to an underworld that can be visited by going through rivers and waterfalls, where other spirit people live. You can find some of these stories in Chapter 4.

Numbers. Cherokee numbers are based on units of ten, like numbers in English. Some numbers have special meaning in Cherokee culture, like four and seven. Four is special because it represents the primary directions—east, south, west, and north. Seven is special because if you take the four directions and add the directions of up, down, and center, you get seven. Many aspects of Cherokee culture come in groups of seven, like the clans. In this book, the stories are arranged in seven chapters to reflect the special meaning Cherokee people give to this number.

Medicine. One Cherokee myth says that animals created diseases for humans, because the humans didn't respect them and were killing too many animals. Plants agreed to help the humans, and they provided a cure for every disease that the animals created. For thousands of years, Cherokees lived in the southern mountains and observed the many things that the plants growing there can do. When Cherokees got sick, their medicine people knew a plant and a remedy for every illness. Did you know that more than half of modern medicines used today were derived originally from plants?

Cherokees also believed it was important to think good thoughts and live in harmony with those around you in order to be healthy. They were very active, spending most of their time outdoors. Traditionally, Cherokee people stayed healthy and cured diseases not only with plants but also by using prayer, steam, good food, and good thoughts.

Growing up. Cherokee language recognizes different stages of life. A baby is called *usdi*, or little one. A girl is *ageyutsa*, and a boy is *atsutsa*. When they are teenagers, girls are called *ata* and boys *awina*. When they become adults, a woman is called *ageya* and a man *asgaya*. An old woman is called *ageyvligei*, and an old man *utvsohnvi*.

Playing and games. Cherokee children and adults played games for fun, and sometimes gambled on them as well. Children played by imitating adults and acting out stories, and they also played many kinds of indoor and outdoor games, some of which included adults. In one, the chunkey game, you rolled a stone along a flat surface, then threw a spear at the spot you thought it would stop. Then you ran and got your spear and stone.

The stickball game was a team sport that was called "the little brother of war." By playing stickball, men learned to watch out for each other, to run fast, to work together, and to fight hard. Each team had a conjurer or medicine man who used magic to try to make the team win. In the game, rules were simple. If the ball was on the ground, you had to use your sticks to pick it up. Once the ball was above your waist, you could use your hands to hold it. Men played hard—tackling, wrestling, hitting, and choking each other, and sometimes someone would be killed in the game. Even so, men were expected not to lose their temper. And afterward, they "went to water" to get rid of any anger or bad feelings toward the other team.

Cherokee towns played stickball against each other, and still do today. Cherokees believe they have played this game forever—going back to the time when animals could talk. A story of how stickball started is included in Chapter 1 of this book, told by Freeman Owle. Versions of this story are told by many Cherokee storytellers.

The Trail of Tears. The U.S. government forced almost all Cherokees and other southeastern American Indians to leave their homes between 1830 and 1840, in order to take their land and resell it to white settlers. They had to walk, in wintertime, about 1,200 miles, from their homes in the Southeast to what was called Indian Territory (now the state of Oklahoma). More than a quarter of the Cherokee population—at least 4,000 people—died on the long walk, which became known as the Trail of Tears.

Cherokee people still live in the mountains of North Carolina, however, because some of them owned land in their own names, some of them hid in the woods during Removal, and some came all the way back from Indian Territory. They worked, earned money, and bought back the land that was originally theirs.

1

Living with **People**

"The Origin of Strawberries"

Cherokee people try to get along with each other, to have a good time and enjoy each other's company without fussing and fighting. Over many centuries of living together they have learned that it's important to get along in order to survive. And it's easier to get along if people don't brag all the time, and if they don't get mad at every little thing, and if they try to help each other.

These stories, passed down orally for centuries, teach children and remind adults about these lessons. Sometimes the stories are about people, and sometimes they're about animals who act a lot like people. Do you know someone who acts like Mr. Possum in the story below?

In the world of these stories, everyone has something to contribute to the community, even if he or she has big feet, like the meadowlark, or new wings, like the bat. Having a sense of humor and being able to laugh at yourself is also an important part of getting along and living in harmony with your friends, family, and neighbors.

✳ The Origin of Strawberries
First Man and First Woman
as told by KATHI LITTLEJOHN

Now,
    how many of you have ever had a fight
    with your brother or sister,
    your best friend or teacher?
Oh no, no, now you better not tell me you had a fight with
        your teacher.
Oh my goodness.
Did—
    before you know it—
    you were yelling ugly mean things
    that you really didn't mean to say,
    mainly about what they looked like and smelled like,
    they were kind of stupid,
    and you hated them,
    and you really didn't,
    but when we get angry
    we say these things without thinking first, don't we?
Well, a long time ago,
    that's exactly what happened between first man and first
        woman.
They were so much in love,
    and they loved one another,
    and they loved their animal friends.
What happened that day
    nobody can even remember,
    but all of a sudden first woman said,

"You are the slowest man on the face of the earth.
I asked you two days ago to help me with this,
and now look what happened."
"Well, you call me slow, you're as slow as an old turtle,"
    he said.
"I asked you if you'd do this,
And not only that, but you're fat," she said.
"Fat, well you're ugly!" he said.
Oh, the ugly things they said about one another,
    and oh, he got so mad,
    and they were yelling and screaming.
First woman burst into tears,
    and she ran out the door.
He ran after her,
    and he hollered,
    "You go on and don't you ever come back."
Oh, and he was still so angry,
    and he stomped around,
    and he thought,
    "She called me fat! Fat? How dare she?
    She ought to look at herself before she—
    Oh, don't you ever come back and tell me that."
Then it got later and later,
    and he got a little more worried about her.
So he went to the edge of the clearing and kinda called her
        name,
    and no answer.
And he thought,
    "That's all right.
    You stay out there all night.
    See if I care."

And he walked back in and slammed the door,
    and it got real late, and real dark.
There were no lights then,
    and he was really worried, and he thought,
    "Gosh, what if something really has happened to her?
    Oh no, oh I can't wait to see her and tell her I'm sorry.
    I told her she was ugly. She's not ugly.
    Oh, I'm so sorry."
And at first light, the next day,
    he started out to try to find where she was,
    and he began to see little signs,
    and he found a broken leaf or a broken branch,
    and he could see the bent grass where she ran.
So pretty soon,
    he started noticing that there was a little flower,
    just about the space of a woman's foot if she was
        running,
    and it was in a straight line.
He'd never seen these flowers before,
    and he followed the little white flowers
    that led him straight to where she was.
She had lain down and gone to sleep.
She stayed right there so he could find her.
He woke her up and said,
    "Oh, my baby, I'm so sorry."
And she went,
    "Oh, smooch smooch honey darlin'."
Oh, mushy mushy.
And they promised they wouldn't fight any more,
    they put their arms around each other,
    and started walking back home, lovey-dovey.

And as they stepped over each of the white flowers,
   they bloomed out into a strawberry.
And the strawberries are supposed to remind us now
   not to ever fight with the people that we care about.
They're just a reminder
   about the first man and first woman's fight,
   and how we got strawberries in the world.

That's how the Cherokee people got the first strawberries.
And the legend goes on to tell us
   that we should keep them in our home at all times:
      maybe a picture,
      maybe jelly,
      it may be strawberry jam.
To remind us not to argue
   as first man and first woman did.

✳ The Origin of the Blowgun
The Old Man and the Birds

as told by DAVY ARCH

This is a story that my grandfather told me
   a long time ago
   when I was just a young boy.
He said that
   way way back before the invention of the blowgun,
   there was an old man who had become old and feeble,
   and he was too old to hunt,
   too old to go to the river and fish,
   he was afraid he would fall on the rocks and hurt
      himself.
All that he was really able to do
   was to go out and tend his garden each day.
And this was the only food that he was able to get for
      himself.
He knew that the vegetables
   and the things that he grew in his garden were good for
      him,
   and they would sustain life,
   but he craved the taste of meat in with his vegetables.
So he prayed
   and asked the Supreme Being if he would help him
   in his quest to have something besides the food he could
      raise in his garden.
So in his dreams that night
   the Supreme Being sent the Little People.
They entered into the dream world of this old man.

In his dream world they showed him how to make a
        blowgun,
    how to fashion the darts.
And they instructed him
    that if he would go out into his cornfields and sit and
        wait,
    the birds that were coming to steal his corn
    would be the victims of the new blowgun that he had
        made.
So the next morning
    when the old man awoke,
    he fashioned a blowgun,
    tied the darts.
It took him a time or two of practice
    before he could get a dart that would fly true.
But he was proud of the invention
    the Little People had taught him to make.
He thought he would try it out.
So he hobbled out into his cornfield,
    sat down still,
    and waited for the birds to come.
Just regular as clockwork,
    here came the birds.
 When they got into the corn
    he was able to shoot them with his new blowgun.
He would take the birds back to his house,
    he would clean the birds,
    wash them good,
    and roast them in front of the fireplace.
He would roast them
    until they were so hard no one could bite them.

They were just like a piece of jerky or dried meat.
He would store these birds and keep them till he needed
      them.
The way he prepared these birds,
  he would take these birds out
  and pound them up in his pounding block that he made
      cornmeal in,
  pound them up into a fine powder.
In the mornings
  when he would make his porridge out of the corn,
  he would season it with some of the birds he had killed
      out of his cornfield.
This was some of the finest food that he had ever tasted.
He began to really enjoy this.
And soon he was eating this every day.
He would season his food
  with the birds that he killed out of his cornfield.
But each day
  he would kill more birds than he needed,
  so he stored these birds in the corner next to the
      fireplace
  where they would stay dry.
This went on for a long time,
  and he was enjoying his food
  and felt the Supreme Being had showed him the way
  he would have meat with his vegetables.
So this went on,
  and one day
  a man passing smelled the birds and the corn soup
      cooking.
And he went over and asked the old man

if he might have some of this fine-smelling food
that he had smelled while passing by his farm.
The old man agreed that he would give him some,
and he sat him down at the table and fed him.
But the man who came by was a thief,
and he looked around
and saw that the old man had all these birds stored in a
corner
next to the fireplace, had big baskets of corn sitting in
the corner.
So the thief thought,
"This old man is not going to live much longer,
he doesn't need all this food,"
so he killed the old man.
And after he had killed the old man,
he ate up what the old man had fixed of the soup
and began to try to prepare his own soup.
But each time that he would try to fix the birds,
he would put the whole bird into the soup.
And every time he would get a bird out to eat,
to put into his mouth,
the bird would change back into a live bird
and fly out of his mouth.
And this was the way that the Little People had of tricking
the thief.
And in the end,
the thief wasn't able to eat any of the food
that he had stolen from the old man.
And in the end,

he starved to death
and he too died,
from killing the old man and stealing his food.

Grandpa was trying to emphasize to me
that you shouldn't do evil for selfish gains,
like the thief that had stolen the old man's food,
thinking that he would be able to eat the food and
survive.
The Little People had put a spell on the food that the old
man gathered,
and each time the thief would try to eat,
the birds would turn back into live birds and fly away.
So he starved to death.
Grandpa was telling me
that bad deeds will return to you,
that the evil you do will come back against you.
The thief should have been thankful for the food that the
old man had given him
and left him in peace instead of doing him the way that
he done.

✳ Medicine & the Wolf Clan

as told by FREEMAN OWLE

In the old days,
    it's said,
    that back in the very, very beginning times,
    after the villages were built,
    it was an old man who came walking out of the woods,
    and he had sores all over his body,
    and he came down to the clans of the Cherokee,
    and he said to the first woman in charge of the first clan,
    "Would you take me in and make me well?"
And she said,
    "Oh, you look so terrible, we don't know how to make
        you well.
    Go away."
The man goes down to another clan of the Cherokee,
    it could have been the Blue Clan,
    and the woman comes out and says,
    "We have children here.
    Don't, don't bother us, please go away."
Again and again
    he's turned away from these villages,
    and eventually he comes to the Wolf Clan of the
        Cherokee.
All the terrible sores on his body,
    and he says to the woman of the Wolf Clan,
    "Will you bring me in and make me well?"
She says,
    "I don't know what to do for you.
    But if you'll come in,

we will lay you down upon the bed,
and we will do everything we possibly can
to make you better."
He went in,
and he lay down upon the bed,
and he sent her out to the forest the first day and said,
"Get the bark of the cherry tree and bring it back and
make tea to let me drink."
And she did.
And his cold went away.
"Go back to the willow tree
and get some bark and make it into a poultice
and wring it and put it upon my sores."
And she did.
And the sores went away.
Again and again for a long time
he sent her into the forest,
telling her every time a certain cure for a certain
ailment.
After a while
he was completely healed.
Then one day he got up from the bed and said,
"Since you were good to me,
I have taught you, the women of the Wolf Clan,
all the cures of the forest.
And from this day forward,
you, the women of the Wolf Clan,
will be the doctors of the communities and the
reservations."

✳ The Bird with Big Feet

as told by KATHI LITTLEJOHN

Have you ever looked in the mirror
    and decided that you wanted to look different?
How would you like to look different?

I wish I was really tall.
I would like to be about six foot tall.
Yeah, I think that would be a good thing.
I would like to be that tall.
I'm five foot five and I would like to be six foot tall.
No, not a giant, I'd just like to be real tall.
I just think that would be a real fun thing to do.
I'd like to be different.

Have you ever looked in the mirror and thought,
    "Gee, I wish I had curly hair,"
    or,
    "Gee I wish I had blonde hair or black hair.
    I wish I looked different."
Do you ever think that?
Well, a long time ago
    there was this bird,
    and this bird was a really nice looking bird,
    except he thought he had too big feet.
Oh, he hated his feet.
He would try to walk through the fields,
    and he'd trip and fall down,
    and all the other animals and the birds would laugh at
        him.

And they'd say,
    "Well, pick up your feet, and you wouldn't do that."
    "Well, if I had feet that looked like yours I'd stay home."
They said mean things about his feet.
And he was very embarrassed about his feet.
One day, he fell down again.
This time when they laughed at him he thought,
    "I can't stand my feet.
    I'm gonna run away and go live
    where nobody can look at me and my feet ever again."
As he was walking away through the field by himself,
    the grasshopper stopped him and said,
    "Where are you going?"
The bird said,
    "I'm sick and tired of my feet,
    everybody laughs at my feet, they point at my feet, they
        laugh.
    I'm gonna go live by myself.
    Nobody's gonna have to look at my feet again."
The grasshopper said,
    "I wouldn't be ashamed of that.
    One day your feet will have a very special purpose.
    Don't worry about your feet."
But the bird didn't listen,
    he just stomped on through the grass by himself,
    and he pouted all day.
The next day,
    there were some men that came to cut down the grass in
        the field
    because they wanted to plant a garden.
What they didn't know was

that there was a bird's nest,
with little baby birds in it,
and if they started cutting down the grass,
they were probably going to kill the baby birds.
The mother bird heard them talking,
and she was real upset.
And she tried to fly away
so that the men would follow her and go away from the
nest,
and they just ignored her.
And then she tried to go and pick up the nest,
and it was way too heavy,
and she might drop the eggs,
and she was just so frantic,
she didn't know what to do.
The grasshopper saw her and said,
"You know, I bet you if you go and ask that bird with big
feet,
I bet you he could help you, and help you move your
eggs."
So she flew over to the field,
and she begged him to come and help,
but he just said,
"Oh not me, I can't help. Why, my big feet!
What if I fell down and I crushed your babies?"
She said,
"Oh no, I know you won't, I know you won't.
Please come and help me. Please."
So he went back with her,
and she got one egg,
and put it on one foot,

and she got the other egg,
and put it on his other foot,
because they were
so big
that they could hold the egg safely.
She got the other egg,
 and together they moved the baby birds on the other
  side of the field.
The men didn't even see them that day, they were safe.
She was so grateful that he had helped her,
 she was so proud of his big feet,
 she went around and told all the other animals what
  happened.
And instead of laughing at his feet,
 they just wanted big feet too.
And that's the legend about the bird with big feet.

✳ The Origin of Stickball
The Story of the Bat
as told by FREEMAN OWLE

Okay. There was a story of a bat.
They say that once there was a dispute between the
        animals and the birds,
   and they were fighting over a certain territory.
And they'd fought for a long time without a great deal of
        settlement of the issue.
And one day the leaders of the group
   decided that they would have a ball game—
   that nothing else was working,
   they were fighting,
   the wars weren't settling anything,
So the ball game could possibly settle the dispute.
So they began to choose their sides.
And the great bear on one side began to choose up his
        team,
   and the eagle began to choose the side for the birds.
And the bear chose
   the mountain lion and the wolf and the bobcat
   and right on down to the chipmunks
   and felt like his side was complete.
But there was a little animal that had been sort of covered
        over by the leaves,
   and he began to run over to the bear,
   and he tapped the bear on his big claw.
And the bear looked down,
   and he said, "Who are you?"

And he said, "I'm a mouse, and I got left out."
And so the bear laughed,
   and he said,
   "You're so small you wouldn't be any good to anybody."
So he kicked the little mouse,
   and he began to tumble and roll through the leaves
   and eventually ended up
   underneath the claw of the great eagle.
The eagle looked down,
   and he said, "What do you want?"

The little mouse said,
  "I'd like to play on your side because the animals don't
    want me.
  The bear has kicked me and mistreated me."
The eagle says,
  "Can you fly?"
The little mouse says,
  "No, I can't fly."
So the eagle summoned the woodpecker,
  and he brought some sycamore bark,
  and he had made holes in it with his sharp beak,
  and they sewed these pieces of bark underneath—
  the wings of the mouse.
And early that morning they began to toss him into the air
  and try to teach him to fly.
All day long he would land with a thud upon the ground.
But eventually,
  late that evening
  just before dark,
  the little mouse learned to fly.
And he flew with such precision that he was great.
They began to toss stones at him
  and couldn't even hit him,
  and he was really, really good.
So the next day
  the ball game began to take place.
They went out to the middle of the field
  as it's traditional to do in the stickball game,
  and they all lined up,
  and they threw the ball up into the air.

And all of a sudden—
  they waited for it to come down,
  and they were going to fight and wrestle
  and fight for the ball,
  but it didn't come down.
And they looked,
  and this little creature had gotten the ball
  before it even came back to the ground
  and had taken it back through the goalposts.
Twenty-one times he scored for the birds.
And the birds won the ball game.
And so if you look out today you'll see him
  just before dark,
  flying,
  and he's called the bat.
There's a great teaching in this story,
  in that
  we should always
  choose all the people
  and not leave out
  those who are smaller.
We should always
  make sure that we don't overlook the feelings of others
  regardless if they're a little bit different than we are.

☀ How the Possum Lost His Beautiful Tail

as told by FREEMAN OWLE

Many stories were told.
Many stories were teaching stories.
The old story of possum was told
    to keep children from bragging and boasting.

The possum was a beautiful creature, but he didn't know
        that.
And one day he was walking out beside the waters
    and looked into the very, very still waters and saw a
        reflection of himself
    and realized that his tail was big and fluffy and beautiful
        and many, many colors.
So he began to admire himself,
    and he walked by that water all day long
    until the wind began to blow.
And then he walked away
    and began to boast and brag to the other animals in the
        forest.
And early every morning he was out
    in the center of the forest
    and waking all the animals up
    to see how beautiful his tail was that day.
Many, many days passed,
    and they began to get tired of it—
    of his boasting and bragging—
    because they knew he was beautiful.

And the fox and the cricket got so tired of it
   that they made a plan to put an end to it.
They had a contest set up in the squaregrounds of the
      Cherokee the next day
   and invited Mr. Possum to come down and participate,
   because it was a contest to see who had the most
      beautiful tail.
And sure, he would do that, he knew he would win, and
      that would be fine.
But they coaxed him into going with them that night
   to comb and brush his tail.
And when he went into the cave of the fox,
   they began to brush his tail and groom it,
   and he began to get a little sleepy.
And as he began to get sleepy,
   they brushed a little faster,
   and soon Mr. Possum was fast asleep.
The cricket, being the creature that he is, began to chew,
   and he chewed *every* hair off the possum's tail.
Well it was not a very pretty tail at that time,
   and they tied it up with a piece of deerskin
   and tied a beautiful bow on the end of it.
And early next morning when the possum awakened, he
      said,
   "What did you do to my tail?"
   being very upset.
And they said, "Oh, we combed and brushed it so
      beautifully
   that we felt like we had to wrap it up
   so it would not get messed up."

And so he was in agreement to that,
    and he bounced on off to the squaregrounds.
And the animals began to go across the stage.
You had the skunk
    with his beautiful black tail
    with a white streak down the middle.
And of course he didn't smell very good,
    but all the people were pleased,
    at a distance.
And the other animals crossed the stage,
    the squirrel,
    and the red fox
    with his big, beautiful orange tail with the black spot on
        the end.
The possum couldn't wait any longer,
    and he began to get antsy.
So he jumped up on the stage
    and he said,
    "It's my time, we need to get this thing settled."
So he said,
    "Take the thing off my tail."
And when they take it off,
    all the animals, and all the people in the audience
    began to roll and laugh and giggle.
And he looks back at his tail,
    and he sees what they're laughing about.
He has the most ugly,
    rat-looking tail
    that he's ever seen in his life.
And first he begins to snarl and spit
    and become very angry.

But after a little while they laugh again
　　and he can't stand it anymore,
　　and he rolls over on his back and he plays dead.
The old possum boasted too much.
And if you go out today
　　and find him in your trash cans,
　　you will see that he begins to snarl like he's going to tear
　　　　you to pieces.
And if you poke him with a little stick,
　　he'll remember
　　that he boasted too much.
And he'll roll over onto his back
　　with all four feet sticking into the air.
And you can pick him up by the tail
　　and carry him back into the forest.
So the teaching of the Cherokee possum story is:
You should let *other* people
　　tell you that you're beautiful.
Don't go around telling everyone else
　　that you are.
Okay?

2
Living with **Animals**

"Getting Fire"

The Cherokees' home in the southern Appalachian Mountains is also home to many kinds of plants and animals: more species in one place than in all of Europe. Cherokees have observed the animals and plants around them very carefully, and many Cherokee stories draw your attention to the special characteristics that distinguish one animal from another—their color, or their markings, or their behavior.

Traditionally, Cherokee people showed great respect for the animals around them, including the ones that they hunted and used for food. A hunter made special preparations of fasting and praying before going hunting. When he killed an animal, he said a special prayer of thanks to its spirit, for allowing it to be used for food to keep him and his family alive. Cherokee people also honor animals by imitating their movements in dances, like the eagle dance, a very serious and beautiful dance that was originally part of ceremonies done only in the wintertime. Today, some Cherokee people still perform dances like these at special events and festivals.

Still another way Cherokee people honor animals is through their stories. In these stories, animals are shown as great helpers that not only provide what people need but also connect people to the world around them.

✳ The Magic Lake

as told by FREEMAN OWLE

I remember these stories because a lot of times at night,
   we were sitting in front of an old wood heater—
   all nine of my brothers and sisters and I—
   having corn.
And I don't know if you've ever done this or not,
   but you'd take a little bit of oil and put it into a frying
      pan,
   and you'd put it on that very hot stove and put kernels
      of corn in it.
They didn't pop but they parched.
Then after a while
   when they got done you could crunch those, and listen
      to these stories.

This young Cherokee boy was walking in the woods,
   and he saw droplets of blood upon the leaves,
   and he began to follow those
   because he was concerned with something being hurt,
   because all the animals were important.
He followed them up the hillside
   and eventually came upon a small bear cub
   who had been wounded, and his leg was bleeding.
And up the hill he went, following the cub, and it would
      stumble and fall,
   and make its way to its feet again,
   and it was struggling, going in one direction,
   to the great mountain that the Cherokees call
      Shakonige,

which is the Blue Mountain
or, today, Clingman's Dome.
And it was a sacred mountain to the Cherokee
and a very special place.
Eventually nightfall came and the bear lay down.
The young man stayed close by that night,
and early in the next morning
the little cub again got up
to go up to the top of the mountain,
and this time made it to the top.
And the fog was covering everything
except for the very peaks of the mountains.
The little cub goes over, and it jumps into the fog.
And the young man says,
"Surely he's gone now."
But all of a sudden
the fog turns to water,
and the little bear begins to swim.
He swims out a ways,
and then he comes back,
and when he gets out of the water,
his leg is completely healed.
And the young man is very confused.
He looks,
and a duck swims in the water with a broken wing,
and his wing is made well.
And animals are coming from all directions
and coming to the water,
and they're swimming and being healed.
He looks up at the Great Spirit,
and he says,

"I don't understand."

The Great Spirit says,

> "Go back and tell your brothers and sisters the
>   Cherokee,
> if they love me,
> if they love all their brothers and sisters,
> and if they love the animals of the earth,
> when they grow old and sick,
> they too can come to a magic lake and be made well
>   again."

✳ The Rattlesnake in the Corn

as told by DAVY ARCH

Seeing corn reminds me of a story
  Grandpa told me about a man that he used to stay with
    named Ute Jumper.
Ute was kind of a medicine man or a conjure man too,
  and Grandpa said that he would stay with him
  a lot of times during, I guess, his teenaged years.
And he said that Ute was all the time amazing him with
    something, you know.
He said one time the corn had got up and was beginning to
      get ripe,
  and Ute told him
  to come with him,
  and he'd show him something.
Said Ute took him up on the mountain
  where his cornfields were at.
Said up above his cornfields
  there was a big rock bar in the mountains,
  in a rough place, with a lot of rocks.
Said when he left
  he'd gotten some milk and some cornbread
  to take with them.
And he said when he got up to this rock bar,
  he called a snake out of the rocks.
Said it was a big yellow rattlesnake,
  said he sang to it
  and fed it this cornbread and milk.
And after he'd fed the snake,
  then he sang to it again

and asked it in Cherokee
  if it would watch his corn for him.
And said the snake went out into the cornfield
  in front of him.
He said when they got out in the middle of the cornfield,
  he sang to it again.
And Grandpa said the snake stayed in that cornfield
  all that fall,
  till they cut the corn
  and got it all in.
And he said that was to keep the rats
  and the ground squirrels
  and the squirrels
  out of the corn.
Said it kept him out of the corn, too!
Said when he was sent after roasting ears
  he'd pick from around the edge!

✳ Getting Fire

as told by KATHI LITTLEJOHN

A long time ago,
    they didn't have fire
    on our side of the world,
    and everything was real dark and real cold.
They knew
    that there was fire on the other side of the world,
    and all the animals wanted some fire.
So one by one
    they said that they were gonna go get the fire.
First,
    the buzzard went.
And he flew way around
    on the other side of the world,
    and he saw some of the fire,
    and he tried to get some.
And he got a real coal,
    a real hot coal,
    and he thought,
    "Great, I got some.
    And I'm gonna fly back
    and take it back on the other side of the world."
And he put it right on top of his head
    and flew off.
And what happened?
It burned off all the feathers on the top of his head.
Oh, it was so hot
    he went and stuck his head in the lake.
And no fire.

Everybody tried.
The little black snake went all the way around on the
          other side of the world,
    (but the snake wasn't even black then).
He stole from the fire.
He didn't have a good place to carry it,
    so he put on the back of his neck,
    and it burnt him black all the way down.
And he's still black.
So he got into the lake to put the fire out.
So he didn't get fire either.

Now they didn't know what to do.
Finally,
    Grandmother Spider said,
    "I may be small,
    but I'm gonna go get the fire."
"You!"
    all the other animals laughed.
"You can't even make it,
    you're so small
    you can't carry that fire."
She said,
    "I might be small, but I'll go get the fire.
    You watch me."
She went all the way on the other side of the world,
    but this time she was thinking,
    "Now, those other animals tried to steal it,
    and it was too hot,
    so I need to put it in something.
    Hmmmm. What can I put it in?"

She went down to the river,
    she made a little pot of clay,
    and she put it on her back.
When she went and got some of the coals,
    the hot coals,
    she put it right in the pot.
She made it all the way back
    and gave everybody some fire.
But then she also gave the Cherokee people the idea of
    making pottery.

3
Living with **Plants & the Earth**

"The Earth"

Cherokee people say they have lived in the southern Appalachians forever. For more than 14,000 years, people have lived in these mountains, according to archaeologists who find their stone tools and skeletons. During this time, Cherokees paid close attention to plants and the earth, and they learned a lot about how plants can be used for food and medicine. They also figured out how to use plants to create shelter, weapons, musical instruments, and cloth.

Today, Cherokee people still believe in showing respect for plants and everything that comes from the earth, rather than taking them for granted. Many of the lessons learned about plants and the earth are passed down today through stories. For example, when Cherokee people gather plants, they don't take the first one they find, but wait until they find at least four plants before gathering any. When they dig a plant out of the ground, they cut off the roots and replant them so another plant will grow. Or they scatter the plant's seeds before they take it, so that more plants will grow in its place.

❋ The Trees Are Alive

as told by EDNA CHEKELELEE

One time I was praying in Cherokee,
   and somebody said,
    "How come you're praying for the trees?"
I said,
   "Cause they're alive.
   Without trees we couldn't make it.
   We wouldn't have no shade
   and feel this clean air."
And I said,
   "That's why
   I always pray for the creatures
   and the trees
   'cause God made us."
And somebody said,
   "Well, He didn't make the tree."
I said,
   "Don't make a mistake,
   He did make the tree.
   He made life, water, and trees."

✳ **Mother Earth's Spring Dress**

as told by EDNA CHEKELELEE

This time of year
    our Mother Earth has worked all winter long
    in making her dress,
    beautiful dress,
    but it's green.
'Bout the early spring she adds some flowers to it.
And whenever she gets ready
    she drops her skirt down the mountainside,
    you can see it across the mountain
    downhill,
    all her skirt is full
    with all the flowers—
    dogwood flowers, azaleas,
    and all kinds of flowers.
That's our Mother's skirt
    that she had worked on all winter long.
So rejoice in it
    and try to keep it clean—
    this is our Mother Earth that we walk on.

✳ The Earth

as told by FREEMAN OWLE

So the Cherokee people still believe that the earth has a lot
      to give.
They still believe that it's important to take care of the
      waters,
  to preserve the air,
  to preserve the forest,
  to preserve the life of people themselves.
When I was a child growing up on the reservation,
  it was not beyond the times of beauty.
It was a time early in the morning,
  when my father would awaken me
  and tell me that it was time to go to the forest.
We would get up before daylight and head to the
      mountaintop.
As we walked, I wondered why.
As I walked, I would sometimes place my foot upon a twig,
  and it would break and snap,
  and he would turn very quietly and say, "Shh."
I would place my feet more carefully,
  and after a while
  I noticed that I was able to place them by feeling where
      they were going,
  without making a sound.
We walked in the darkness for a long time and finally came
      to a clearing,
  and I noticed the beautiful stars in the sky early that
      morning.

And he said,

    "Sit down."

I sat down upon the ground,

    and I began to look at the beautiful heavens,

    and after a while I began to hear noises, all around.

And he said,

    "Be quiet."

There was a noise off to the left,

    then a noise in the front,

    and then the leaves were rattling in the trees up to the
        right,

    but I remained still.

After a while,

    the rays of sunlight began to take over the skies,

    and the stars disappear.

The rays of sun revealed to me

    that off on the right were squirrels jumping in the
        hickory nut trees,

    revealed to me

    that in front of me in the forest there was a deer, with
        its baby,

    and off to the left the grouse was shuffling in the leaves
        with baby chicks.

And no sooner had the sun come,

    than my father said,

    "We're ready to go."

We got up from the clearing,

    and we walked out of the forest,

    and in my mind was a question of

    why that we had done this.

But after I returned home,
  he told me,
  "What have you learned?"
I said,
  "I've learned, Father, that if you're quiet enough,
  still enough, long enough,
  that you become part of nature."
And he said,
  "You've learned well, son."
He loved the forest.
He loved to tell the stories of the Cherokees.

✳ Corn Woman Spirit

as told by FREEMAN OWLE

This story gives some respect to the women in the tribe.
There's a story of the Corn Woman.
And she is a spirit that is sent down from heaven every
      year
   to come and walk in the fields of the Cherokee.
And when she walked in the fields
   the corn began to grow,
   and it grew tall and beautiful.
The Cherokee corn is a corn that is very, very special,
   because it is a corn that has ten rows of kernels on it.
And most other ears have thirteen,
   that we are familiar with today.
So the Cherokee corn will grow almost ten feet tall,
   and on those stalks it will have three or four ears of
      corn,
   where most other kinds of stalks have one or two,
   and it's beautiful in color.
It's all the colors of the rainbow.
And many people ask, "How did you paint that?"
The Cherokees ate it.
It's a very good corn.

Anyway, this Corn Woman would walk in the fields,
   and the corn would grow beautifully.
One year they planted their corn
   and had gone out to watch it come up,
   and it didn't come up.

And they waited a week,
    and then two weeks,
    and it still hadn't come up.
So they prayed to the Great Spirit
    and asked where the Corn Woman Spirit was.
And he said that he had sent her down two weeks before,
    but she was missing.
And so the people began to look.
And they looked all over the earth known to them at that
        time,
    and they couldn't find her.
So they began to ask the animal kingdom
    if they would help search for her.
So all the animals were searching for this beautiful Corn
        Woman Spirit
    when all of a sudden the raven dived down into a dark
        cave
    and was looking for her.
And he found her in the bottom of the cave, all tied up.
She was captured and prisoner
    of the evil spirit Hunger.
And he was dancing around her and laughing,
    knowing very well that if she didn't get out,
    that the Cherokee people would starve the coming
        winter.
So the raven went back and reported to the people
    that he had found the Corn Woman Spirit.
And they told the raven
    that only he and his family could get her free.
So they told him to go down into the cave

and perch on the ledges
and hide from the evil spirit,
and he did.
He took all of his brothers and sisters into the cave,
and they were so black they couldn't be seen by the evil
spirit,
and they perched on the ledges and the rocks.
When the signal was given they all leaped down
and pecked the evil spirit
and made such terrible noises
that they frightened him out into the sunlight.
And like most evil,
when he hit the sunlight he just melted away
and disappeared.
They freed the Corn Woman Spirit with their big strong
beaks,
and when she walked out into the sunlight
the corn of the Cherokees began to grow.
From that day forward, the Great Spirit in the heavens
would not let her come down in person.
And so it is today.
So when you look out at the cornfields
and see the stalks of corn
and their leaves waving in the wind,
you'll know that the Corn Woman Spirit
is walking though the fields of today.

Cherokees are unlike the Appalachian people,
they don't take the raven
and hang him up on a stick and expect the other ravens
to understand,

"Well I can't go to that field, that raven ate corn and he
     was killed."
That wouldn't stop them.
The Cherokees give the raven a very special place:
     that he was the one that saved the fields of the
          Cherokee.
So therefore they feel that if he takes a few kernels of corn,
     that's OK.
But if the raven is in the field, and an animal comes into
     the field,
     the crows and the ravens will pitch such a fit
     that the people will know
     that someone is stealing their corn,
     so they can go down and chase them away.
So I imagine it's all in the way you look at animals and the
     circle of life
     as to whether they're necessary or need to be destroyed.
The Cherokee saw the importance of all animals and all
     people
     and so therefore they had a very special place.
And that story, I feel, is told to teach those lessons.

✳ A Medicine Story

as told by ROBERT BUSHYHEAD

When I was a little boy
   I believed in Creator,
   the Great Spirit.
And all the created things were
   a part of the creation,
   and they spoke.
Like my daddy, when he was raising corn,
   in the evening he would say —
   late in the evening he would say,
   "I must go into the field and talk to the corn."
He had what people called a green thumb.
Everything that he planted
   always came up good
   and yielded much fruit.
And so that was his term:
   "I must go now and talk to my corn."

And then, of course,
   whenever medicine was needed,
   again they would turn to nature.
The medicine man
   did not go out
   and pick herbs, roots, or barks at random.
He went because he knew
   the Great Spirit would lead him.
And I remember one time
   that a close relative of mine,

in fact my aunt,
    came to the house.
And the medicine man had sent her out
    to gather some medicine for a sick person.
She said,
    "Bob, I want you to go with me."
And I went with her.
And on the way to the hillside,
    she explained to me what kind of an herb
    or what kind of a plant
    we were looking for.

And I knew the plant well,
   and when we came to the woods,
   I saw a lot of plants that she had described to me,
   and I knew that was the plant.
And I said,
   "There's one!"
And she came over,
   and she looked at it,
   and she said,
   "No, that's not the one."
Yet I knew and realized
   that that was the plant she had described.
So I didn't say anything,
   just kept on going with her,
   knowing that she had something else
   that I should learn.
And maybe it was because she wanted me to learn
   that she took me along with her—
   I realized that later.
And whenever we were along the hillside,
   I saw many, many plants like the one she had described
      to me,
   and each time she would say,
   "No, that's not the one."
And then after a while,
   she said,
   "Bob, come up here.
   There's the plant."
And it was the same species of plant that I had been
      showing to her,

and she had said, "That isn't it."
So I went on up there,
    and I saw the plant,
    the same kind I had been pointing out.
But this time
    this particular plant
    was shaking.
    There was no breeze, but
    that plant was trembling.
And she said,
    "That's it, that's the one."
And so by that
    you know she had some kind of spiritual guidance
    as to find which plant she was looking for.
And then
    she carefully dug the root out of that ground.
And the plant—
    when she broke the root from the plant,
    she shoved that plant back into the ground
    after she had removed the root.
And then she said,
    "We have to be sure,
    we have to be sure,
    because the sick person is depending on us,
    the medicine man is depending on us to get the right
      herb."
And so she said,
    "Let's take it down to the creek."
And we took off from the hillside
    down to the creek,

and she took that root and washed the dirt off of it.
And then she put that root in the palm of her hand
   and stood there
   just for a minute or so.
And without any encouragement,
   the root turned over in her hand.
And she said,
   "That's it. That's it."
And then she took that root back to the medicine man,
   and the medicine man worked with that root
   and prepared that root,
   and the patient got well.

So I guess maybe it was a lesson that she wanted me to
      learn:
   that you just don't go out into the woods and pick herbs
      at random.
You name the person,
   but as you're naming the person,
   you have to know what clan they are:
   the Wolf Clan, the Deer Clan, or the Paint Clan,
   or whatever clan that they might be,
   and there are seven.
And you have to know the clan of the patient you are
      treating,
   because you're asking for this medicine from the Great
      Spirit,
   and he directs all of your movements.
And that plant was for that particular man and particular
      clan.

And so I think that
    during this time
    the Indian looked to nature for guidance
    in all the activities of his undertakings.
I think that I can verify
    just the thing that we have been talking about
    as being true,
    because it happened to me at one time.

4

Living with **Spirits**

"Nunnehi, the Gentle People"

Cherokee stories describe spirit warriors, ghosts, mischievous Little People, and the immortals who live in a world alongside ours. Other people around the world also tell stories about supernatural events, but the particular beliefs of the Cherokees make their stories different. In Cherokee stories, events always happen in specific places, and certain places are considered doorways to other worlds.

Traditionally, Cherokee people believed in one God, the Creator, who made everything. But they also believed in spirits, ghosts, and Little People. The Nunnehi and the spirit warriors of Nikwasi Mound are believed to be, as Kathi Littlejohn says, "always with us." These invisible beings live alongside regular Cherokee people, and may appear in this world in order to help in times of trouble. Ghosts, however, are the spirits of people who have died, and may cause trouble.

Little People also live alongside Cherokee people. They are only rarely seen, but they do live in this world. They may play tricks on us. Cherokee people believe that if you are walking outside and see something you want to pick up, like a rock or feather, you should first ask the Little People if it belongs to them. If you feel that they're saying it's OK to take it, you still must leave something in return. If you don't, they will come to your house and take something in exchange. This is why things sometimes seem to disappear and you can't find them!

✳ **Spirit Warriors & The Nikwasi Mound**

as told by FREEMAN OWLE

Nikwasi was down on the valley of the Tennessee,
  and all of a sudden
  people known as the Creeks began to come up and
    attack
  and threaten to destroy the village of Nikwasi.
The Cherokee people rallied,
  they came to protect the village,
  but over and over again the Creeks came in greater
    numbers,
  and eventually the Cherokees were losing, very badly.
And they'd almost given up,
  when all of a sudden the mound of Nikwasi opened up,
  and little soldiers began to march out of this mound by
    the thousands.
And so they go out and they defeat the Creeks,
  and like in biblical times
  they kill all of the Creeks except for one.
And he goes back and tells the other Creek brothers and
    sisters,
  "Never ever mess with the village of Nikwasi,
  because they have spirit people who protect it."
And never again
  was this village attacked by the Creeks.

Later, during the Civil War time
  the Yankee soldiers came down from the north,
  and they were camped out

and ready to come down and to burn
the little town of Franklin, North Carolina.
They sent scouts down to Franklin, North Carolina,
and the scouts went back telling their commanding
officer,
"You can't attack Franklin, North Carolina.
It is heavily guarded, there's soldiers on every corner."
And the soldiers went around,
toward Atlanta, Georgia, and burned everything in the
path.
But Franklin, North Carolina, was not touched.
But the history and the reality was
that every able fighting person had left Franklin to fight
in the Civil War.
There were no men here.
The old Cherokees say it was the Nunnehi, the Little
People,
that again protected
Franklin, North Carolina.

✳ **Santeetlah Ghost Story**

as told by EDNA CHEKELELEE

I was born back in Santeetlah
   where Joyce Kilmer Memorial Forest is now.
And I used to walk to school in Snowbird,
   and we used to walk to go to church,
   fourteen miles round trip.
People walked everywhere in those days,
   over the gaps in the mountains.

This is a ghost story.
Somebody had passed away,
   and my daddy said we had to go sit up,
   'cause they believed in sitting up all night;
   when somebody died,
   one of their relatives,
   they'd sit up all night long,
   they wouldn't sleep.
So he said, "We're going to have to go."
So we left,
   I think it was right around eight o'clock in the evening.
When we got the news, it was seven,
   so it was eight o'clock, probably, when we got ready
      to go.
We crossed the river,
   and we had big rocks that we jumped over
   to get across,
   so we crossed over,
   and we started climbing up the hill.
And nothing but laurel bush and moonlight,

that's all we could see,
    going up the trail.
As we walked the trail, I was behind my mother,
    and she was walking in front of me,
    and then I grabbed her skirt and hanged on to it
    'cause I was always afraid of the dark.
'Cause I used to listen to the old people,
    when they would sit on the porch,
    and lean back in their chairs
    and tell stories.
They would tell some ghost stories,
    and there was one ghost story I was always afraid of,
    and thought, sure enough, there must be ghosts.

So we was walking on the trail,
    and as we walked up
    I heard something make a whistling sound.
And I said,
    "Daddy, what is it?"
And he said,
    "Oh, don't worry about it, everything's okay."
And I keep hearing it getting closer.
I said,
    "Daddy, it's getting closer, what is it?"
It would whistle, whistle,
    low like that,
    so it must have been a-breathing,
    that sound that I heard.
Anyway, I got close to my mother, and I closed my eyes,
    and I kept hearing something behind me.
Then I got between my mother and dad,
    in the middle,
    and I closed my eyes tighter.
And then finally I peeped a little bit,
    and I saw something white behind me.
And as we walked up, Daddy said,
    "Everything's going to be all right.
    Don't get scared.
    Don't ever get scared.
    If you don't get scared, everything'll be okay."
So—I couldn't help but shake.
But I thought I would just keep walking.
Finally Daddy said,
    "Okay, everybody stop.
    Get back up on the side.

Let that thing go through
in front of us."
I said,
"What is it?"
He said,
"Oh, that's okay, I'll take care of it."
So we stood back on the side,
on a bank,
and I kept hearing
chomping on the leaves,
and it would breathe heavy like that.

And I peeped,
opened my eyes like that,
and I saw nothing but a
sheer
white
cloth
looked like a clinging curtain,
and it didn't have no head,
no shape over the head,
all I saw was the shoulders.
So he was standing right on the side,
and Daddy said,
"All right."
He said,
"You've scared my children enough,"
said, "I just about know who you are,"
said, "go on ahead and step ahead,
I don't care about you."
Said,

"Go on ahead, and step ahead.
You're not going to hurt my children,
and I'm not going to hurt you.
Just go on by, we made room for you to go by."
And all at once we heard a little bit,
and it was just chompin' up the leaves.
All at once I closed my eyes again,
and I kept hearing—
and I just shook.
Finally I opened my eyes
a little bit like that,
and here he was going up in the air—
no feet,
and all I could see was sheer cloth
climbing up the laurel bushes like that.
And finally just went on
through the laurel bushes,
and it faded away.
And Daddy said,
"He's gone, he left us alone, so don't worry about it.
Don't ever get scared, everything'll be okay."

So ever since then I feel much better about being in
the dark.
I'm still afraid of the dark sometimes!
But just remember, if you're not afraid,
a ghost can't hurt you.
If you get afraid and panic,
you might run over a cliff or fall and hurt yourself.
But if you're not afraid,
a ghost can't hurt you.

The Cherokee Little People — Forever Boy

as told by KATHI LITTLEJOHN

There are a lot of stories and legends about the Little
      People.
You can see the people out in the forest.
They can talk, and they look a lot like Indian people
   except they're only about two feet high,
   sometimes they're smaller.
Now the Little People can be very helpful,
   and they can also play tricks on us, too.

At one time there was a boy.
This boy never wanted to grow up.
In fact, he never wanted to grow up,
   and told everyone that so much
   that they called him "Forever Boy"
   because he never wanted to be grown.
When his friends would sit around and talk about:
   "Oh when I get to be a man, and when I get to be grown
   I'm gonna be this and I'm gonna go here and be this,"
   he'd just go off and play by himself.
He didn't even want to hear it,
   'cause he never wanted to grow up.
Finally his father got real tired of this,
   and he said,
   "Forever Boy, I will never call you that again.
   From now on you're going to learn to be a man,
   you're going to take responsibility for yourself,
   and you're going to stop playing all day long.

77

You have to learn these things.
Starting tomorrow, you're going to go to your uncle's,
and he's going to teach you everything that you need to
    know."
Forever Boy was brokenhearted at what his father told him,
    but he could not stand the thought of growing up.
He went out to the river and he cried.
He cried so hard
    that he didn't see his animal friends gather around him.
And they were trying to tell him something,
    and they were trying to make him feel better,
    and finally he thought he understood them to say,
    "Come here tomorrow. Come here early."
Well, he thought they just wanted to say goodbye to him.
And he drug his feet going home.
He couldn't even sleep, he was so upset.
The next morning he went out early, as he had promised,
    to meet his friends.
And he was so sad,
    he couldn't even bear the thought of telling them
    goodbye forever.
Finally
    he began to get a sense that they were trying to tell him
    something else,
    and that is to look behind him.
And as he looked behind him,
    there they were—
    all the Little People—
    and they were smiling at him and laughing and running
    to hug him.

And they said,

"Forever Boy, you don't have to grow up.

You can stay with us forever.

You can come and be one of us and you will never have
to grow up."

"I can't do that. I have . . . my uncle's waiting on me.

I can't do that. It would hurt my parents if I never came
home again."

And they said,

"No, we will ask the Creator to send a vision to your
parents

to let them know that you are safe and you are doing
what you need to do."

Forever Boy thought about it for a long time.

But he decided that's what he needed to do.

And he went with the Little People.

And even today

when you're out in the woods and you see something,

and you look, and it's not really what you thought it
was,

or if you're fishing and you feel something on the end of
your line,

and you think it's the biggest trout ever,

and you pull it in,

and all it is is a stick that got tangled in your hook,

that's what the Little People are doing.

They're playing tricks on you

so you'll laugh and keep young in your heart.

Because that's the spirit of Little People, and Forever Boy,

to keep us young in our hearts.

✳ Nunnehi, the Gentle People

as told by KATHI LITTLEJOHN

If you ever go out into the woods,
    and you think you hear someone talking,
    maybe some music,
    and you know there's no one else around you,
    there's a reason for that.
Out in the woods there live the gentle people.
And we call them the Cherokee word:
    Nunnehi.
The Nunnehi look a lot like Cherokee people,
    only they live underground
    in a special, special place.
One time, the Nunnehi came to the Cherokee people,
    and it was a very big surprise.
The Nunnehi men came to the head village and said,
    "You're going to have to come with us now.
    All of you pack up your belongings,
    and in seven days
    you will have to come with me
    and come and live with the Nunnehi."
Well, you can imagine what everyone was thinking.
"Why?"
"Where are we going to go?"
"Why do we have to go?"
"I don't want to go."
"Well, I want to go."
And they argued back and forth for days
    about what was going to happen.
They asked him on the seventh day

where they were going and why.
He said,
    "Something terrible is going to happen.
    Worse than any flood
    or any famine
    that you have ever known before.
    Some dark and terrible day is coming,
    and you have to leave now to save yourselves."
Well, when he said that,
    they decided to go with him.
So they packed up all their belongings,
    and they followed him for miles
    until they came to a big stone way deep in the
        mountains.
And as they watched, the stone rolled away.
They rushed to the entrance to see what was beyond
        there—
    to see where they were going.
And it was the most beautiful place that they had ever
        seen.
The most beautiful place that they could imagine.
The air just seemed to dance with joy.
It was beautiful.
Without even looking back,
    many families rushed ahead.
And as they turned to close the door forever,
    they saw a group standing way in the back.
The chief went over and asked them,
    "Why aren't you coming in?
    We're getting ready to close the door.
    You have to come now."

But the old people in the group said,
"We were born here,
　　and no matter what happens we want to stay."
The young people said,
　　"We want our children to be born
　　here in the mountains
　　where our grandparents were born.
　　And we've decided to stay."
He was torn between going with this group and staying.
He decided that he needed to stay,
　　that whatever bad was coming,
　　he needed to stay and help lead his people.
The stone rolled over,
　　and we've never seen or heard from them again.
The others remained,
　　and these are the ones that we're descended from.
The bad part
　　was the Trail of Tears removal
　　that forced thousands of people to leave this area and go
　　　　to Oklahoma.
So if the Nunnehi ever come again,
　　we know something bad is going to happen
　　and will have to decide what to do then.
Remember that as you're out in the woods
　　you might hear something,
　　you might hear some music,
　　you might hear someone talking,
　　and it's the Nunnehi,
　　and they're reminding us
　　that they're always with us.

5

Living with **Monsters**

"Spearfinger"

The Cherokee landscape was full of monsters, giants, spirits, and Little People. Some lived in specific places, while others haunted all the Cherokee towns and the mountains. One story says that a giant inchworm lived in the Nantahala Gorge until Cherokees killed it. A giant yellow jacket once terrorized Wayah Gap. A giant man, Judaculla, was a legendary hunter who lived in the rough high mountains between the Tuckaseegee River and the Pigeon River, where a bald and a gap are named for him. The cave where he lived, according to legend, is now called the Devil's Courthouse. A giant snake, the *uktena*, was as big around as a man's body, with antler's like a deer and a large crystal set in its forehead. It was so poisonous that just its gaze could kill people.

Here you'll find the story of Cherokee children's favorite horrible monster, Spearfinger. The story of the Hunter and Thunder tells how a hunter saved someone from the *uktena*, and in return, received the power to turn thunderstorms away and keep them from destroying crops. Because of this, Cherokee people sometimes refer to themselves as Friends of Thunder.

✳ Spearfinger

as told by KATHI LITTLEJOHN

Have you ever watched a real scary movie?
Were you scared?
No?
What about when you went to bed and turned off the
            lights,
      did you look under the bed for monsters?
No?
How 'bout your closet?
Did you hear your dog outside and think something had
            come to get you?
Well, you have to remember that those monsters are not
            real.
Turn on your light at any time, and the monsters are gone.
It's just in our imagination.

But a long long long time ago,
      those monsters were real.
And the worst one
      that the Cherokee people had
      was called
      Spearfinger.
She was awful.
She was forty feet tall,
      and she was covered with this rock-like skin
      that no bullet, no weapon could penetrate.
And she was bloodthirsty.
She had one long,
      razor-sharp,

spear finger,
    that she would slip up behind you,
    slip it through your back,
    pull out your liver,
    and eat it in one gulp.
She was covered with dried blood
    and snot, and gore dripped from her teeth.
She had razor-sharp teeth,
    she was vicious,
    and she was always coming around.
She loved to eat the flesh of young children
    more than anything.
And to get close to the children,
    she could change her shape.
She could turn and look just like your sister,
    just like your granny.
And as you were out picking blackberries
    or fishing or playing,
    your friend could disappear,
    and she would take his place,
    and you'd never know it until it was too late.
One day
    this village not far from here
    knew that Spearfinger was getting close to them.
And they just panicked.
    "What are we gonna do? Just let her walk in here and eat
        everybody?"
    "Well, I think we ought to fight her."
And they argued back and forth,
    "No, not me, I think we ought to run."
So they finally came up with a plan,

that they would dig this huge pit
all the way around the outside of the village
and cover it over with branches and trees and bushes,
and when she fell into it,
then they would try to kill her.
Everybody started helping.
They started digging,
    and everybody started helping,
    and moving rocks and getting the bushes.
And a young man,
    about your age,
    was really trying to help.
He was a little bit clumsy,
    'cause he was real excited.
He was trying to help,
    and he'd go to pull this, and he'd fall down.
He'd run get a big bucket of mud,
    and he'd spill it.
Finally,
    his dad got real aggravated with him
    and said,
    "Just go over there and sit.
    If you can't do any better than that, just get out of the
        way."
Oh, this really hurt his feelings,
    'cause he was just trying to help.
    "Golly, those little babies there, nobody's yelling at
        them, they fall down."
And he went over,
    sat underneath the bushes,
    and he was just very upset.

He thought,
    "Spearfinger's coming,
    we all need to help,
    and nobody even wants to talk to me."
He felt real sorry for himself.
And he noticed
    that there was a little bird
    that was stuck in a honeysuckle vine
    and couldn't get loose.
But he was still real upset,
    and not even thinking about the bird,
    he just gently let it loose,
    and was very surprised when the bird didn't fly off.
Instead,
    the bird came right on his shoulder
    and said,
    "I really thank you for helping me,
    and I'm gonna tell you a secret about Spearfinger.
    I know where her heart is."

And the boy said, "She doesn't have a heart.
    You can't shoot her through the heart because it's all
        covered with rocks.
    Even our strongest warrior can't shoot through that."

"No," she said,
"The birds follow Spearfinger, and we know all of her
        secrets.
We know where she hides,
we know where her heart is

'cause she doesn't fool with trying to eat us, we're too
    small.
Look at the tip of her spear finger,
and that's where her heart is.
Shoot her there."

Oh, that boy was so excited,
    and he ran, and he said,
    "Dad, dad, dad, I know where her heart is."
The dad said,
    "I told you to get over there and sit down.
    I don't want to hear it."
And he ran over,
    and he tried to tell his mom,
    but before he could even tell anybody,
    they heard a horrible scream through the forest.
And it was Spearfinger.
And she was coming fast,
    and she was ravenously hungry.
Oh, she was screaming,
    and they ran and hid,
    and she fell into the pit,
    and they ran,
    and they started trying to kill her,
    threw rocks at her,
    and she was just clawing her way up to the top.
Blood was just foaming at her mouth.
She was nasty.
And she was awful.
They knew that if she got loose she would kill everybody.

So they were trying to shoot her,
　　shoot with bows and arrows,
　　and they were screaming and running and trying to hide.
The little boy ran up to the strongest warrior and said,
　　"Look at the tip of her spear finger."
And he looked,
　　and it was just about as big as that,
　　just tiny, just tiny.
But he drew back
　　and shot her right through the heart,
　　and she fell over dead.
And after that the little boy was a great hero.
Everybody listened to him after that day.

✳ The Hunter & Thunder

as told by ROBERT BUSHYHEAD

Now we should go back to the hunter and the thunder and
      the serpent.
A hunter,
    he was treated by the medicine man while he was still a
      baby
    to be successful.
And then to know,
    to understand the ways of nature so far as animals are
      concerned.
And he went out several times,
    many, many times,
    to feed the family,
    to feed the whole village sometimes.
And so he was very successful.
Hardly ever did he come home without anything.
But one day,
    he went out,
    he had no success.
No success at all in any form.
And around about noon
    he sat down
    under a tree
    and was sitting there
    when he heard a call:
    "Help me, help me, help me."
And as a hunter
    he had keen ears;

he was trying to get the direction
from which the sound came.
He paused,
    and when he reached the top of the hill,
    he looked down in the valley.
And there in the valley was a man,
    and this man was saying,
    "Help me, help me, help me."
A snake was coiled around him, and
    squeezing, squeezing, squeezing,
    until that man's voice was very weak.

And when the hunter approached him,
  the man said,
  "Help, help, help."
And the serpent said,
  "No, help me, help me,
  let's kill this man."
And the man said,
  very faintly,
  "Do you want to help me?
  Shoot this snake on the seventh spot on his neck."
Well, you know,
  the hunter didn't have very much choice,
  he chose to help the man.
And he put his arrow into his bow,
  and with a twang the arrow left the bow
  and went straight to his mark
  into the seventh spot on the serpent.
And it began to uncoil,
  and it fell dead.

Then the hunter went and helped this man up
  and stayed with him.
And the man said,
  after he stood there a few minutes and got his strength
    back,
  said to this hunter,
  "Let's go over to the top of the hill,
  I'll have something to tell you."
They went on up the hill and sat down,
  and the man said,

"My name is Thunder,
and you can refer to me as Uncle,
and you did me a great favor today.
Now, I like to destroy things,
I like to have fun.
But if there's anything that would hurt you,
all you have to do is talk to me."
And he gave him a formula,
gave him the formula for protection, see.
Well, anyway, my mother knew this formula,
When a storm came up
you've seen storms rising,
black clouds mixed with white clouds,
you know, coming in your direction.
When that would happen,
she would say,
"Boys, be quiet,
sit over there in the corner."
And then she would stand at the edge of the porch,
I could tell she was saying something.
And this storm was coming,
and she was worried about her crops;
they were near the harvest stage.
And then she would stand on the porch
and say this formula.
Then she would go blow right into the middle of an
oncoming storm,
blow this way,
and then she would say the formula again,
and this time she would blow that way.

And after a while
　　after seven times,
　　she said it seven times,
　　and then after the seventh time,
　　we would see a little clear spot
　　formed in that part of the storm
　　where she blew this way,
　　in that part of the storm
　　she blew that way.
Now if somebody just told me that,
　　I wouldn't know whether to believe it or not.
But I saw it.

So the storm would miss us.
The storm would move around
　　the crops that she was trying to protect.
Many, many are the things that we have seen.

6

Living with **Cherokee Language**

"The Origin of the Milky Way"

Cherokee people have spoken their language for thousands of years. It could be extinct within twenty years, though, because most of the people who grew up speaking the language are more than fifty years old. The Cherokee tribes in North Carolina and Oklahoma are trying hard to keep their language alive. They are sponsoring immersion classes for babies, where fluent speakers talk to them all day long, so that they will grow up speaking the language as if they learned it at home.

Cherokee people want to keep their language alive because they feel it makes them Cherokee. Their language is unique among Amcrican Indian languages in the southeastern United States. It is related to the languages spoken by Iroquois people in New York state and the Great Lakes region.

A Cherokee man, Sequoyah, invented a system of writing for his language. He could not read and write in any language, but he worked for twelve years to create this system that represents the sounds of Cherokee language in eighty-five syllables. According to Cherokee legend, while he was studying the language, he neglected his farm and his blacksmithing and silverwork. His wife thought he was crazy and burned all his papers at one point. His neighbors thought he was practicing witchcraft, making strange marks, and burned his house down. But he kept on, with the help of his daughter Ayoka. Finally, in 1824, the Cherokee National Council recognized Sequoyah's form of writing and created a silver medal in recognition of his accomplishment. Other American Indians have also invented forms of writing for their languages, beginning with the Olmecs in 750 B.C. in Mexico. Sequoyah's syllabary has become a source of pride and a symbol of identity for the Cherokee people.

The story of the Origin of the Milky Way was told by Swimmer in about 1888 to James Mooney, who wrote it down. Many Cherokee people know and tell this story today. Marie Junaluska translated it into Cherokee language. You can see it in phonetics and in Sequoyah's syllabary following the English version of the story.

✳ Cherokee Language

as told by EDNA CHEKELELEE

Repeat after me:
  Siyo.
A little louder:
  Siyo.
You said "Hello."

Osigwotsu osigwotsu.
You said, "How are you?"

Osigwo, osigwo
All right!
Now, you learned my language.

I learned your language when I was five years old.
I had to, regardless if I wanted to or not.
When I went to school we were told that we had to learn
    one way or another
If I didn't learn I had to go to the bathroom,
    wash my mouth out with Ivory soap.
But I never did wash my Indian language out,
    I still got it in my heart,
    and I still carry on my Indian language.

✳ The Origin of the Milky Way

as told by SWIMMER, *about 1888*

Some people in the south had a corn mill,
    in which they pounded the corn into meal.
And several mornings when they came to fill it
    they noticed that some of the meal had been stolen
    during the night.
They examined the ground
    and found the tracks of a dog,
    so the next night they watched.
And when the dog came from the north
    and began to eat the meal out of the bowl,
    they sprang out
    and whipped him.
He ran off howling
    to his home in the north,
    with the meal dropping from his mouth
    as he ran.
And leaving behind a white trail
    where now we see the Milky Way,
    which the Cherokee call to this day
    Gili uli sv sda nvyi,
    "where the dog ran"

⁂ Gili Ulisvdanvyi

as translated by MARIE JUNALUSKA

Tsuganawv iditsa anehi igada yvwi
  selu asdosdi nunvhne,
  selu unihsdosdi selu itsa nanvnehei,
  halviyuwalidi dagitsvhvsgv widanilanidohv (selu)
    anadelohosge
  ganosgida gesv selu ihtsa svnoyi iyvhi.
Eladino unigoliyee,
  dunigohe gili dulasinvsdanv,
  nahiyu sunaleiyv ulisihvsa unagisesdane,
  tsuhyvtsv iditsa diyuloshv gili ulutsa,
ulenv ulisdayvna selu itsa unvwedv galodvi,
  tsunanelugise unilivnilei.
Tsuhyvtsv iditsa tsuwenvshv wulishvsdane
  wuweluwadise utsewotsehe uhnvsgalv selu ihtsa,
  wudanvne unega wulosv nasgi goiyv
  gili ulisvsdanvyi tsawidigowatisgoi,
nasgi Anitsalagi "gili ulisvsdanvyi"
  tsanosehoi goiyvhi.

ᎩᎵ ᎤᎵᏒᏓᏅᏱ

ᏧᎦᎾᏮ ᎢᏗᏣ ᎠᏁᎯ ᎢᎦᏓ ᏴᏫ ᏎᎷ ᎠᏍᏙᏍᏗ ᏄᏅᏁ, ᏎᎷ ᎤᏂᏍᏙᏍᏗ ᏎᎷ ᎢᏣ ᎾᏅᏁᎮᎢ ᎭᎸᎢᏳᏩᎵᏗ ᏓᎩᏒᎲᏍᎬ ᏫᏓᏂᎳᏂᏙᎲ (ᏎᎷ) ᎠᎾᏕᎶᎰ ᏍᎨ ᎦᏃᏍᎩᏓ ᎨᏒ ᏎᎷ ᎢᏣ ᏒᏃᏱ ᎢᏴᎯ. ᎡᎳᏗᏃ ᎤᏂᎪᎵᏰᎡ, ᏚᏂᎪᎮ ᎩᎵ ᏚᎳᏏᏅᏍᏓᏅ, ᎾᎯᏳ ᏑᎾᎴᎢᏴ ᎤᎵᏏᎲᏌ ᎤᎾᎩᏎᏍᏓᏁ, ᏧᏴᏨ ᎢᏗᏣ ᏗᏳᎶᏒ ᎩᎵ ᎤᎷᏣ ᎤᎴᏅ ᎤᎵᏍᏓᏴᎾ ᏎᎷ ᎢᏣ ᎤᏅᏪᏛ ᎦᎶᏛᎢ, ᏧᎾᏁᎷᎩᏎ ᎤᏂᎵᎥᏂᎴᎢ. ᏧᏴᏨ ᎢᏗᏣ ᏧᏪᏅᏒ ᏭᎵᏒᏍᏓᏁ ᏭᏪᎷᏩᏗᏎ ᎤᏤᏬᏤᎮ ᎤᏅᏍᎦᎸ ᏎᎷ ᎢᏣ, ᏭᏓᏅᏁ ᎤᏁᎦ ᏭᎶᏒ ᎾᏍᎩ ᎪᎢᏴ ᎩᎵ ᎤᎵᏒᏍᏓᏅᏱ ᏣᏫᏗᎪᏩᏗᏍᎪᎢ, ᎾᏍᎩ ᎠᏂᏣᎳᎩ "ᎩᎵ ᎤᎵᏒᏍᏓᏅᏱ" ᏣᏃᏎᎰ Ꭲ ᎪᎢᏴᎯ.

7
Living with **the Past & Future**

"The Trail of Tears"

Cherokee stories tell about historical events in the past, like wars and heroic deeds. At one time the Cherokees dominated more than 140,000 square miles—parts of eight present-day states. During the 1700s the Cherokees made treaties with European nations and their colonies. The British, French, and Spanish, as well as the Virginians and South Carolinians, all wanted to have the Cherokee warriors as their allies and wanted to trade with Cherokee men and women for their valuable deerskins, baskets, and corn.

But in the 1800s, the new United States wanted more land, and the government removed American Indians from their homelands all over the country, sending them to Indian Territory, now the state of Oklahoma. The Cherokees resisted this by getting deeds to their land, creating a bilingual newspaper to state their position, signing a petition, and finally taking their case to the U.S. Supreme Court, which decided in their favor in 1832. The United States removed them anyway, in 1838, forcing them on a long march to Indian Territory that became known as the Trail of Tears. At least one-quarter of the Cherokee people died on this forced march of more than 1,200 miles.

Some Cherokee people managed to stay in their original homeland in the mountains of North Carolina, where about 13,000 members of the Eastern Band of the Cherokee Nation live today. Through wars, diseases, invasions, and forced removal, the Cherokee people have survived. These stories look to the past and to the future.

✳ The Trail of Tears

as told by FREEMAN OWLE

As I was growing up,
    my parents began to tell me this story of the Trail of
        Tears.
You look at me and you say,
    "Well, he's probably the same as I am."
Yes, I am. I am Cherokee and I am also Scots-Irish.
But I am *Uguku tsiskayi Tsalagi askaya.*
My name is Owle, I live in Birdtown,
    and I happened to grow up on the reservation.
My Cherokee family was, in 1838, in a log cabin near
        Murphy, North Carolina.
And all of a sudden,
    someone was banging on the door
    early that morning.
And they opened up the door and they looked out,
    and fifty Georgia soldiers were standing in the yard.
They said,
    "Come out of the cabin."
And when my great-grandfather—
    I'll just call him grandfather—
    did,
    they burned the cabin to the ground.
He and his wife and small baby were taken to Murphy,
        North Carolina,
    put into a stockade,
    stayed there for six weeks.
There was no roof, only a line of poles
    encircling the stockade.

They say that
  the mud was deep,
  there wasn't much food,
  no one had anything to cover themselves with,
  but the baby survived because the mother was feeding it.
Early one morning,
  on that October morning
  when the frost was heavy
  and the ground was frozen hard enough for wagons to
    travel,
  General Winfield Scott began to march the people out of
    this fort.
So he marched them across the frozen ground
  and across the Santeetlah Mountains
  into Tennessee.
They began to march on toward Oklahoma.
When they got to the Mississippi, they asked my
    grandfather
  if he would count the Cherokees who crossed the river.
And he said,
  "Yes, I will."
But he told his wife in Cherokee,
  "Go hide in the canebrake and take the baby with you.
  And I will tell them you're here.
  And we'll go back home."
So he counted the Cherokees as they crossed the flatboat
    across the Mississippi,
  and he told the soldiers,
  "All the Cherokees are accounted for."
And they said,

"Are you sure?
Go back to the river and check again."
And this was what he wanted,
    and he goes back to the river,
    and he looks into the bushes and the brush,
    and all of a sudden he leaps into the water.
They come running behind, and they shoot many times
        into the water.
They look into the black, swirling waters of the
        Mississippi,
    and this Cherokee doesn't surface.
So they look for a long time.
And they give him up as being dead.
He's breathing through a reed all this time.
And after he gives the soldiers time enough to go away,
    he comes up and he swims back
    across the Mississippi.
He looks for his wife on the other side,
    and—she heard the gunshots.
She ran
    with the baby in her arms,
    she would run all night long,
    and then find a briar patch to sleep in in the daytime,
    or a farmer's haystack.
Took her several weeks to get back home,
    but she came on back to the old burned-out cabin site
    because that's all she knew as home.
She waited there week after week,
    and her husband didn't return.
She went down to the village,

to the Scots-Irish settlers,
and they gladly gave her food.
And they were feeding those Cherokees
that were hiding in the mountains.
If the North Carolina settlers had been caught
handing out food to the Cherokees,
they too would have lost their land and been put in
prison
as Cherokee sympathizers.
But the Scots-Irish people were feeding her
one morning, a year later,
when she heard a noise up on the hill,
and she looked and there was someone coming.
And so she ran and hid with the baby.
And after a while it was her husband
coming out of the woods.
They were reunited,
and we still live
in a little place where they came and rebought with
their own money
called Birdtown.
And the reason they were able to rebuy it
was that Chief Yonaguska adopted a white child
who grew up to be a lawyer,
William Holland Thomas.
He was a citizen of the United States,
and the Cherokees were able to go and buy up land
and put it in his name, by the thousands of acres.
And we are still here.

I want to tell you
    that the Cherokee people don't really hold any hatred
    or animosity in their heart
    for those things that happened in the past.
The reason the Cherokee people survived
    is because they loved their neighbors
    and were good neighbors.

✳ Removal

as told by DAVY ARCH

Solomon Bird is a man I know in Robbinsville.
And I went to visit him a few summers ago,
   took my grandfather down there
   and Mike Kline, who was working as a folklorist up at
   Western Carolina University, was with us.
And it was really funny.
Mike had gone to visit Solomon on an occasion before we
      went.
And Solomon had used his granddaughter as an interpreter,
   and wouldn't speak English to Mike.
So Mike thought that Solomon couldn't speak English.
So it was funny, when we got to his house that day,
   he came out
   and he knew that I didn't speak enough Cherokee
   to communicate in Cherokee.
And Grandpa is more comfortable with English now than
      he is Cherokee,
   even though he does speak it fairly fluently.
Realizing this, Solomon, when he came out,
   just started talking in English,
   and Mike's mouth just fell open.
He was really floored by it.
But Solomon told us a story that day,
   of his grandmother,
      who had lived on the road where he lived,
      on up the road there.
And when the soldiers came through and rounded up the
      people,

they had taken his grandmother and her parents
at gunpoint
and marched them down the road,
    right in front of Solomon's house.
And you know, to hear him talk about that,
    and relate the story that his grandmother told him
        about that specific place right there in front of his
            house.
It was really a touching thing and caused me to realize
            how —
    how close, that this had happened not so long ago.
It was recent history
    and not prehistoric,
    things that we kind of generalize about,
    that this was a true story.
His grandmother had stayed captive for three days
    before they had escaped and come back up into that part
        of the country
    there in Little Snowbird.
And there was a lot of people like that, I think, who were
        rounded up.
And this valley, that goes up the Oconaluftee River here,
        was very populated,
    there was a huge town through here.
And they came in and rounded everybody up at gunpoint
        and marched them out.
And this was something that I don't think a lot of
        Cherokees were aware of.
I think a lot of people didn't have a whole lot of
        communication
    with what was going on at the time

and so they were totally taken by surprise, a lot of them,
    I think.
And children—
    like Solomon's grandmother—
    had no idea what was going on.
It was just a very traumatic scary time.
They thought they were all going to be killed
    because they all knew the stories
      of the British coming through and exterminating the
        villages.
So these,
    when the army came in with guns to march them out,
    I'm sure these stories about the atrocities that had
      happened in the past
    just kind of flashed to their minds.
And the worst things imaginable
    probably were really preying on these people's minds.
And some really catastrophic things did happen
    to a lot of people that were rounded up.
Now Solomon, when he told the story, really conveyed a
    lot of emotion.
This was something that he felt was a crime that had been
    committed
    against him as well as his grandmother
    because of how she told him the story.
So there still are a lot of people who still remember the
    Removal that clearly.

☆ ☆ ☆ ☆
    ☆
112   ☆
      ☆

✳ The Legend of the Corn Beads

as told by EDNA CHEKELELEE

Cherokee women
   wear the legendary necklace made of corn beads.
It is a gift
   from the Great Spirit
   in the shape of a teardrop.

This is the Cherokee legend of the corn beads.
In the 1800s
    during the Trail of Tears,
    the corn stalk were eight feet tall,
    and corn was twelve to eighteen inches long.
The corn stood back and watched
    as the Indian people were getting pushed and shoved
    by the white soldiers.
And the corn cried and cried.
And the teardrop landed on the corn fodder,
    and the corn dropped down to three feet tall.
That's why it's called teardrop,
    our mother of corn.
The Cherokee women used these teardrops,
    our mother of corn,
    to make beautiful corn beads,
    but to me this is sad.
But it is a way to remember
    the Trail of Tears.

✳ People Singing in the Earth

as told by FREEMAN OWLE

Long before the tragedies of the people happened,
    the Cherokees were sitting in a council house.
You can imagine this big building sitting on top of a
        mound
    with thousands of seats inside.
And they're all gathered in the middle of winter,
    and there's a big fire crackling in the middle of the
        council.
And the chiefs are all gathered
    in the center,
    at the bottom,
    and the people are listening
    to the oral history being told
    or to the business being discussed.
When all of a sudden
    with no wind whatsoever outside
    the bearskin on the council house opens up
    wide enough for a person to come through
    and then sort of folds back,
    and then all of a sudden
    drops back into place.
The Cherokee, being very superstitious
    as they were in those days,
    realized that someone, some spirit,
    had entered the council house.
So they sat very quietly,
    and sure enough, up in the corner of the council house
    they began to see a light.

A sort of greenish-colored light materialized,
   and it soon turned into a person.
They knew this person was a Cherokee,
   but they didn't know who he was.
He came down to where the chiefs were sitting,
   and he said,
      "You, my brothers and sisters, must follow me.
      For out of the east will come a group of people
      who will destroy your homes.
      And your villages will be burned,
      and your children will be killed,
      and your homeland will be taken away,
      and never again will you be happy."
And so the Cherokees said,
      "No, we can't leave,
      because this land belonged to our mothers' mothers'
         mothers."
He said,
      "I'll be back in seven days,
      and you must fast and decide
      whether you'll go with me
      or stay here and suffer."
In seven days he came back again,
   and half of the people had decided to follow him,
   half had decided to stay home.
And so when he came,
   the half that followed him
   went up toward the mountain,
   the sacred mountain of the Cherokee.
And he got to this great massive rock cliff

and he touched it with his hand,
and the whole cliff opened up.
And you could hear people singing and laughing inside the
    mountain,
and a stairwell leading up to a beautiful land
of springtime and summer.
The people began to march in
with the butterflies flying,
and the fruit trees bearing fruit,
and the people were all happy.
One man at the end
decided that—he had left his family there in the village,
and he wanted to go back and get them
and bring them to this beautiful land.
He rushed back to the village
and headed back to the mountain.
When he got back to the mountain with his family
the mountain had closed up,
and they said he was crazy
and left him there alone.
He stayed there for seven days,
and on the seventh day
he began to hear the singing
deep within the earth.
And so he went back to the village.
And from that day forward
he told the people in the village
that if you're quiet enough,
    long enough,
and if you sit and listen to the streams

and really are aware
and very quiet and still,
that you too can hear the people singing within the
    earth,
    those happy ones that went on before.
And sure enough, the settlers came,
    and they began to burn the villages
    and take away the land.
And the Cherokee people have been searching
    for that happiness
    they had long, long ago.

And I think the teaching of this story
    not only was the fact that there was a revelation
    of what was about to happen —
    people losing their homeland
        on the Trail of Tears and so on.
But also to teach us
that we should never let the child disappear from us.

You remember when you were a child,
    when you would take off your shoes
    and prod through the mud puddles
    and laugh and sing?
Remember when you were a child,
    that not a butterfly passed
    that you didn't see it and chase it?
And not an animal or an insect were overlooked,
    that you were so close to nature
    and so close to Mother Earth
    that those were the things that were important to you?

We should remain like children
   and sometimes take our shoes off
   and prod through the mud puddles
   and sit by the streams
   and listen to the talking of the streams
     and the whispers of the wind.

We must preserve the earth,
   and we must value the lives of our elders
   and the lives of our children
   and save them a place to live.
If we don't
   then there will be a revelation for the people of today
   as well as for the Cherokee.

Glossary

bird with big feet. Meadowlark.

blowgun. A Cherokee weapon used to hunt birds and small game, consisting of a long river cane tube through which darts are blown. The Cherokees did not put poison on the darts.

clan. A group of people related through their mother. Cherokee clans are Wolf, Deer, Bird, Paint, Wild Potato, Long Hair, and Blue.

conjurer. A magician who heals people or makes bad things happen to people.

council house, townhouse. A building at the center of a Cherokee town large enough to hold everyone who lives in the town. It was often built on top of a mound.

Creator, Supreme Being, Great Spirit, Unehlanvi. Cherokee names for God. Cherokees believed in one God who made everything.

formula. A special prayer used by conjurers and medicine people.

Little People. Small supernatural beings who may play tricks on people or help them.

medicine man, medicine woman. A person who uses plants and prayers to heal people.

mound. A large mound of dirt created in the center of Cherokee towns. Some were as much as forty feet high. On top of the mound stood the townhouse, where people met to make decisions, tell stories, dance, and conduct ceremonies.

Nunnehi. Supernatural beings who live in a world alongside ours.

pounding block, corn pounder. A section of log set upright, with the top hollowed out, in which corn is pounded into cornmeal.

Qualla Boundary. A large tract of land bought back by the Cherokees after Removal. It consists of about 57,000 acres (about 100 square miles) west of Asheville, North Carolina, in the Great Smoky Mountains, where they lived before Removal.

Removal. U.S. government action taking all American Indians out of the Southeast between 1830 and 1840.

stickball. A traditional Cherokee game, played by two teams, called "the little brother of war." The winning team is the first to score twelve points by getting the ball through the goal posts at the other team's end of the field. Players use sticks with a small net on one end to scoop the ball up from the ground. They can touch the ball with their hands only if it is above their waists. They can tackle, wrestle, choke, and hit their opponents in advancing the ball. The night before the game, the conjurer of each team leads ceremonies and dances to help his team win by magic. This game, played in different forms by many Indian tribes, was the basis for the modern game of lacrosse.

Trail of Tears. The forced march of the Cherokees 1,200 miles from their homeland to Indian Territory (now Oklahoma). The Cherokees called it "the trail where they cried," referring to the people who cried in sympathy as they saw the Cherokees pass through their towns.

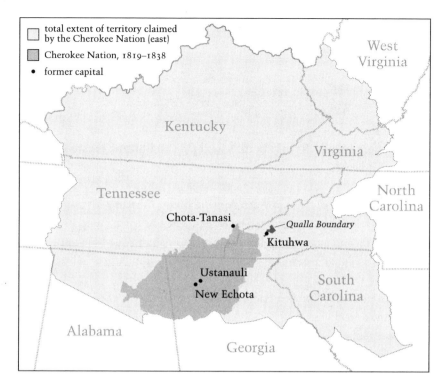

Cherokee Lands (adapted from a map by Brett H. Riggs).

Timeline

12,000 B.C.

People live in the southern Appalachians, hunting mastodons with spears.

8,000 B.C.

People live in the southern Appalachians, hunting with spears and atlatls and fishing in the rivers. They begin growing gourds and sunflowers and trading their soapstone bowls to people as far away as the Great Lakes and the Gulf of Mexico.

2,000 B.C.

Cherokee becomes a language different from other Iroquoian languages.

1,000 B.C.

Cherokee people live in permanent villages along rivers and creeks throughout the southern Appalachians. They begin making pottery.

500 A.D.

Cherokee people begin hunting with bows and arrows. Many of their towns have a central mound with a council house on top.

800

Cherokee women develop their own kind of corn and grow it in large fields.

1200

Cherokee women develop unique kinds of beans and grow them along with corn and squash.

1540

An expedition led by Spanish explorer Hernando De Soto comes through Cherokee territory.

1600s

Many Cherokee people die from diseases introduced from Europe.

1700

Cherokees begin trading with the British and French.

1756–59

Cherokees fight as allies of the British against the French in the French and Indian War.

1760–61

The Cherokee War—Cherokees vs. the British.

1762

Cherokee leaders go to London and meet with King George III to make peace.

1776–85

Cherokees fight with the British against the Americans in the Revolutionary War.

1789–1839

Cherokees follow George Washington's "Civilization Policy," creating schools, a written language, a police force, a supreme court, Christian churches, and a model capital city at New Echota, Georgia.

1794

Dragging Canoe and the Chickamauga Cherokees surrender after fighting twenty years for Cherokee land.

1814

Cherokee warriors help Andrew Jackson defeat the Creek Indians in the Battle of Horseshoe Bend during the War of 1812.

1824

Sequoyah's system of writing is recognized by the Cherokee National Council.

1838

The U.S. government forces the Cherokees to leave their homeland and march to Indian Territory.

1868

The Eastern Band of Cherokee Indians is recognized as a tribe by the U.S. government. They elect a new chief and draw up a written constitution.

1889

The Eastern Band of Cherokee Indians is recognized by North Carolina as a corporation.

1917–18

Cherokee men fight in World War I.

1930

Eastern Cherokees get U.S. citizenship through a special act of Congress.

1941–45

Cherokee men fight in World War II. Some are "Codetalkers" in their units, using Cherokee language as a secret code to confuse the enemy.

1946

Eastern Cherokees are allowed to vote in national elections.

1996

Cherokees elect the first woman chief of the Eastern Band, Joyce Dugan.

1996

The Eastern Band of Cherokee Indians buys back the Kituhwa Mound.

2007

The Eastern Band of Cherokee Indians buys back Cowee Mound.

Further Reading

Bell, Corydon. *John Rattling-Gourd of Big Cove: A Collection of Cherokee Indian Legends.* Written and illustrated by Corydon Bell. New York: Macmillan, 1955.

Bradley, Ramona K. *Weavers of Tales.* Cherokee, N.C.: Qualla Arts and Crafts Co-op, 1967.

Bruchac, Joseph. *The First Strawberries: A Cherokee Story.* Retold by Joseph Bruchac. Illustrated by Anna Vojtech. New York: Dial Books for Young Readers, 1993.

Bruchac, Joseph, and Gayle Ross. *The Story of the Milky Way: A Cherokee Tale.* 1st ed. New York: Dial Books for Young Readers, 1995.

Burrison, John A., ed. *Storytellers: Folktales and Legends from the South.* Athens: University of Georgia Press, 1989.

Chiltoskey, Mary Ulmer. *Aunt Mary, Tell Me a Story: A Collection of Cherokee Legends and Tales.* Cherokee, N.C.: Cherokee Communications, 1991.

Conley, Robert J. *Mountain Windsong: A Novel of the Trail of Tears.* Norman: University of Oklahoma Press, 1992.

Duncan, Barbara R., ed. *Where It All Began: Cherokee Creation Stories in Art.* Cherokee, N.C.: Museum of the Cherokee Indian Press, 2001.

Duncan, Barbara, ed.; with Davey Arch, Robert Bushyhead, Edna Chekelelee, Marie Junaluska, Kathi Smith Littlejohn, and Freeman Owle. *Living Stories of the Cherokee.* Chapel Hill: University of North Carolina Press, 1998.

Duvall, Deborah L. *How Medicine Came to the People: A Tale of the Ancient Cherokee.* Drawings by Murv Jacob. Albuquerque: University of New Mexico Press, 2003.

Kilpatrick, Jack Frederick, and Anna Gritts Kilpatrick. "Eastern Cherokee Folktales: Reconstructed from the Field Notes of Frans M. Olbrechts." *Anthropological Papers No. 80, Bureau of American Ethnology Bulletin No. 196*. Washington, D.C.: Smithsonian Institution, 1966.

Mooney, James. *Myths and Sacred Formulas of the Cherokees.* Cherokee, N.C.: Cherokee Publications, 2006.

Ross, Gayle. *How Rabbit Tricked Otter, and Other Cherokee Trickster Stories*. New York: Harper Collins, 1994.

About the Storytellers

Traditionally, a Cherokee person becomes a storyteller by first hearing stories from his or her family and community. Someone who hears and learns to tell stories in this way uses the same words, rhythm, and tone of voice as the grandparents and elders who, in turn, learned these stories from their grandparents and elders. More than just the words are passed on. Someone who learns to tell stories in this way, who has grown up in a Cherokee family and community, understands how these stories relate to Cherokee life and belief, to a particular sense of humor, and to a long history of people living together in a certain way.

There are wonderful Cherokee storytellers among the people of the Eastern Band of Cherokee Indians as well as the Cherokee Nation and the United Keetoowah Band in Oklahoma. The storytellers whose tales are included here are just a few of the people who keep the Cherokee storytelling tradition alive.

DAVY ARCH was born in 1957 on the Qualla Boundary. He is a storyteller, a lecturer on Cherokee history and culture, and a mask carver. Sometimes his masks illustrate the stories he tells. Davy learned many of his stories from his grandfather and others in his family. He explains that Cherokee people have used storytelling to teach each other about living together in the world and to pass on their history. Davy learned many stories like the ones here because elders shared them with him in the evening, often after an evening meal.

ROBERT BUSHYHEAD was born in 1917 near Cherokee, North Carolina, and passed away in 2001. He grew up speaking only Cherokee in his home, until he went to boarding school and was forced to speak English. He worked as a minister and also spent many years gathering information about the kind of Cherokee language spoken around Cherokee, called the "Kituhwa dialect." During his life, he was honored with many awards.

EDNA CHEKELELEE was born in the Snowbird Community in western North Carolina in 1930, and passed away in 1995. She was descended from a famous Cherokee man: Junaluska's brother, Wachacha. Together, in the nineteenth century, they fought with Andrew Jackson at Horseshoe Bend to defeat the Creek nation. Later they helped Cherokee people stay in the Snowbird Community even through Removal and the Trail of Tears.

Edna taught Cherokee language, dances, and arts and crafts to many young people in her community. She sang gospel music with her mother. She loved to cook, and she adopted and fostered many children. She traveled all over the country sharing Cherokee culture with people.

MARIE LAMBERT JUNALUSKA grew up speaking Cherokee language. She has translated old articles from the first Cherokee newspaper, the *Cherokee Phoenix*, into English as part of her work as a translator for the Tribal Council of the Eastern Band of Cherokee Indians. In this book, she translates a story told more than a hundred years ago by a Cherokee man named Swimmer, whose songs, stories, and medicine formulas were written down by James Mooney at the end of the 1800s.

KATHI LITTLEJOHN was born and raised in Cherokee, North Carolina. She learned to tell stories when she worked at the Oconaluftee Indian Village and Living History Museum, where visitors can learn about traditional Cherokee ways of life. On days when the weather was bad, and few visitors came through, the older people would sit and talk, telling traditional stories to the younger people. Now Kathi shares her stories with her children and stepchildren. She also tells stories in public with her husband Leroy Littlejohn, who tells stories in Cherokee language. Together they have been helping to create materials for Cherokee language classes for children as young as two or three years old.

FREEMAN OWLE was born in 1946 and grew up in the Birdtown Community on the Qualla Boundary. He became a schoolteacher but now travels around the country educating people about Cherokee history and culture by telling stories. He learned to tell stories from his family, often while they sat together around an old woodstove in their home. He also makes stone carvings that tell stories.

Acknowledgments

My thanks continue to go to the storytellers who shared their stories in the original edition of *Living Stories of the Cherokee* (1998) on which this new edition of stories for children is based: Davy Arch, Robert Bushyhead, Edna Chekelelee, Marie Junaluska, Kathi Littlejohn, and Freeman Owle. Robert and Edna have passed away, but their stories and their families live on. Thanks also to Shan Goshorn for the illustrations in the book and for her inspired cover art.

As Cherokee artists and storytellers, these people are making the culture live for their generation, and for generations to come. I am honored to be a small part of this process. *Itsilielitsesi.* I appreciate all of you—you make me happy.

To my children, John Harper Duncan and Pearl Louise Duncan, love always.

I am thankful to my friends and family—Bernadine, Bullet, Carolyn, Donna, cousin KJ, Loanne, Roberto, Shan, Shirley, my sister Susan, and Tommy P; Ken, Sharon, and folks at the Museum of the Cherokee Indian; my neighbors on Camp Creek; the warriors of AniKituhwa; and Charles, Katherine, and Annie Frazier.

I appreciate the comments of teachers who have requested this edition for young readers over the past ten years, and I'm glad that it has finally come to be. Thanks to David Perry and Mark Simpson-Vos at the University of North Carolina Press for seeing the vision and then guiding the process that created this edition.

Thanks also to my daughter Pearl's fourth grade class at East Franklin Elementary for talking with me and sharing their thoughts about these stories and their questions about the

Cherokees in May of 2004. I'm grateful for the time I spent with Kaley Alexander, Jonathan Anderson, Michael Antes, Allie Brendle, Dillon Cabe, Aaron Coin, Courtney Collier, Karey Conner, Brittany Croston, Pearl Louise Duncan, Tiffani Dyer, Scott Elliott, Ana Florida, Lydia A. Hanson, Thomas Hartley, Melanie Khioukhom, Cody Lindley, Kuteka Lopez, Jessica Mallonee, Zachary McCall, Lacy Millsaps, Shannon Pena, Valerie Queen, James Savis, Jerry L. Shepherd Jr., Rashaune Stevens, and their teacher, Mrs. Crystal Parker. Did you know it takes a long time to make a book? But not as long as the time it took to make these stories.